Praise for *What Should I Say to my Friend?*

"The church needs men who love the local church, who believe that theology matters, who want to influence another generation, and who have a heart to get the Gospel to the ends of the earth. Tom Elliff is one of those men. This little book is a starting point to help reach non-believers and train believers around the world."

⸲ **CHUCK LAWLESS**, DEAN OF BILLY GRAHAM SCHOOL, VICE-PRESIDENT FOR ACADEMIC PROGRAMMING, THE SOUTHERN BAPTIST THEOLOGICAL SEMINARY

"My friend, Tom Elliff, has delightfully explained profound truth through a story that will become a classic for training witnesses at home and abroad. The most basic Bible doctrines are simple, interesting, and memorable. This unforgettable story gives doctrinal depth to making disciples, and I couldn't put the book down!"

⸲ **AVERY WILLIS**, EXECUTIVE DIRECTOR OF INTERNATIONAL ORALITY NETWORK, FORMER VICE PRESIDENT FOR OVERSEAS OPERATIONS OF THE INTERNATIONAL MISSION BOARD, SBC

"Dr. Tom Elliff has used his gift of communication and deep biblical insight to train missionaries in basic doctrinal foundations for several years. *What Should I Say to My Friend?* provides the reader with a simple narrative that explains essential doctrines effectively. Not only does it help the reader understand doctrine, but it is a valuable tool for any believer to learn how to share God's redemptive purpose."

⸲ **JERRY RANKIN**, PRESIDENT OF THE INTERNATIONAL MISSION BOARD, SBC

What Should I Say to my Friend?

Tom Elliff

Copyright ©2009 by the International Mission Board
All rights reserved.
Printed in the United States of America

ISBN: 978-0-9767645-4-0

Published by the International Mission Board, Richmond, Virginia

Dewey Decimal Classification: 239
Subject Heading: APOLOGETICS AND POLEMICS

Scripture taken from the NEW AMERICAN STANDARD BIBLE®
Copyright ©1960,1962,1963,1968,1971,1972,1973,1975,1977,1995
by The Lockman Foundation. Used by permission.

Cover and interior design: Rick Boyd, BOYDesign

Editor: Kim P. Davis, Richmond, VA

*Dedicated to
the faithful participants and staff
of the
International Mission Board's
Field Personnel Orientation,
with gratitude to God
for the passionate manner
in which they pursue their calling
to the ends of the earth.*

Contents

Foreword
1

Introduction
3

Chapter One
What Should I Say to my Friend about God?
7

Chapter One Review
21

Chapter Two
What Should I Say to my Friend about the Bible?
23

Chapter Two Review
32

Chapter Three
What Should I Say to my Friend about Man and the Problem of Sin?
33

Chapter Three Review
43

Chapter Four
What Should I Say to my Friend about Jesus, God's Answer for the Sinner?
45

Chapter Four Review
58

Chapter Five
What Should I Say to my Friend about Faith?
59

Chapter Five Review
70

Chapter Six
What Should I Say to my Friend about the Church?
73

Chapter Six Review
89

Chapter Seven
What Should I Say to my Friend about Baptism and the Lord's Supper?
91

Chapter Seven Review
106

Chapter Eight
What Should I Say to my Friend When I am at a Loss for Words?
107

Afterword
111

Discussion Questions
113

Foreword

ONE OF THE GREATEST PRIVILEGES OF MY LIFE came by way of an invitation to teach essential doctrines of the Christian faith to outbound missionaries of the Southern Baptist Convention's International Mission Board (IMB). To this day, I continue to savor the joy of sharing on that vital topic with such eager and dedicated individuals. Little can compare to the exhilaration experienced when addressing an energized assembly of newly called and committed missionaries, ready to take the Gospel to the whole world and ready to spend all and spare nothing.

People primarily think of missionaries in terms of their evangelistic enterprises. Leading people to a saving faith in Jesus Christ, however, is only one part of the Great Commission challenge. Of course, we are to make disciples (not mere converts), and we are to lead them to that moment of open commitment of faith, as symbolized by baptism. But there is more—much more, in fact.

Physicians are quite concerned about the care a patient receives immediately following a surgical procedure. They know that the patient's future welfare is at stake during those first few days and weeks following surgery, and they do all they can to facilitate good health and strength by urging a change in the patient's lifestyle. Similarly, new believers in Christ have received a spiritual heart transplant. Their future health and effectiveness is best enabled as they learn to do all that Christ commanded those first disciples. Wherever possible, the teaching and enabling aspect of the Great Commission is best accomplished through the extended ministry of the local church. In fact, the New Testament model reveals that the most effective mission efforts were accomplished by, in, through, and with the support of local churches.

Missionaries sent out by their local churches are then to be both evangelists and church planters, with a special interest and passion for the people groups in this world that have yet to be reached. They must have something more than a keen sense of "those things most surely believed." They must possess some capacity for transferring those truths to others of like faith and kindred spirit. It is out of that concern that the material in this book was first presented in lecture fashion to outbound missionaries of the IMB.

I want to thank the Lord for those who have been so helpful in providing me both the opportunity and the setting for teaching essential doctrines to our outbound missionaries. Elbert Smith, Chuck Lawless, Kim Davis, Dan Allen, Rick Boyd, Jill Shanks, and Nancy Robertson gave me valuable counsel regarding cross-cultural witnessing, doctrinal verities, and matters of language and style. I am especially grateful for Dr. Jerry Rankin's invitation to work alongside the executive officers of the IMB and for every individual who serves as part of our IMB team, most especially those who serve at the Baker James Cauthen and Eloise Glass Cauthen International Learning Center.

Rejoice evermore!
Tom Elliff
2 Timothy 1:12

Introduction

THIS SMALL BOOK IS NOVEL IN ITS APPROACH—quite literally. On one hand, it is a compact collection of teachings on seven essential Christian doctrines. On the other hand, these teachings are rendered as a narrative. You will follow the life of a young university student as he seeks to communicate his faith in a strange culture. His experience is sometimes overwhelmingly exciting and joy-filled. At other times, you will find him discouraged, disillusioned, and fearful.

For several years, I have used the title "What Should I Say to my Friend?" for a series of lectures on essential Christian doctrines presented to outbound missionaries. My goal has been to solidify in their minds the importance and relevance of doctrinal studies. For many people, the term *doctrine* is fraught with ideas of pedantic, often boring and impractical teaching, coupled with the demands of memorization. Nothing could be further from the truth!

A solid grasp of basic Christian doctrine is more than an absolute necessity for the serious follower of Christ; it is the gateway to effectiveness, certainty, and boldness in fulfilling the task. Martyrs, after all, were never put to death because of their feelings. It was their firmly held beliefs that brought them into conflict with their culture. So we had better be sure what we believe and why we believe it!

I also have used the theme of this book to remind outbound missionaries of the simple truth that we are in the communication business. Someone once said that the Gospel is good news as long as it gets there in time. I would add that it is more than the mere arrival of a missionary on foreign soil that makes the difference. The Gospel is only Good News for those to whom it is told.

With the above in mind, I have sought to share a simple method by which any individual can communicate the truth regarding seven essential doctrines of the Christian faith. These are conversations you can have with your friends, family members, and neighbors anytime and anywhere. By following the pattern modeled for you in this book, you will be able to give sufficient answers when asked about:

1. The nature of God
2. The Bible or the source of truth
3. Mankind and the problem of sin
4. Jesus, God's provision for our salvation
5. Faith and what it means to "believe"
6. The church, its gifts and its mission
7. The meaning of baptism and the Lord's Supper

Of course, these are not the only essential doctrines of the Christian faith, but they are the issues that seem to be raised most often by individuals who have serious questions regarding the Christian faith and the practices of a local church.

Sufficient versus complete

You will quickly grasp the fact that I am not dealing with each of the above doctrines in a complete fashion. That would be as impossible in this short book as it is in the brief course that I teach to missionaries. My concern here is not so much a *complete* answer but a *sufficient* answer. For this reason, you will find that these doctrines are approached in a fashion that is remarkably simple, if not elementary. It would be an embarrassment, in fact, to say so *little* about each of these doctrines, were it not for the fact that these are simple suggestions for communicating truth to individuals who have virtually no grasp of the Christian faith. Thus, I must emphasize that this approach is not at all incorrect, but the serious student will find it incomplete.

One Scripture to memorize

I must also address another issue regarding a teaching method I have employed when speaking to missionaries about these essential doctrines. It is this method that guides the general format of this book. Since our goal is a sufficient answer rather than a complete answer, it is often helpful for us to focus our attention on a single Scripture verse or passage that will in itself serve to frame an appropriate response. I have encouraged missionaries to memorize a single Scripture verse or passage associated with each of these essential doctrines. Additionally, I have sought to model for them a legitimate method for "unpacking" that passage, letting it speak for itself. When questioned about a particular belief, it is then a relatively simple task to recall the Scripture and let it fall open as a mental guide when responding to a doctrinal question. While it is not necessary to verbally quote the Scripture passage, the very fact that you have memorized it and know how it unfolds to address a doctrinal issue can serve to guide you in your discussion.

Over the years, I have often employed alliteration as a tool for memorization. You will frequently see the use of alliteration on these pages as well. I want to do everything possible to aid you in both the memorization and the application of the truths found in the Word of

God. At first, it may seem a bit trite to employ alliteration in a book on essential doctrines. But if your friend does question you concerning one of the doctrines in this book, and if you can recall both the Scripture and an appropriate manner for dealing with it, the tool will have served its purpose.

Now, it's time for you to meet Bill and his friend.

What Should I Say to my Friend about God?

Chapter One

For from Him and through Him and to Him are all things. To Him be the glory forever. Amen. (Romans 11:36)

THE TRAFFIC SURGED FORWARD INEXORABLY, like the murky waters of a great canal, swirling occasionally around the inevitable accident or streaming outward like a tributary into an adjacent thoroughfare. Tumbling along like flotsam in that river of transport was an odd assortment of vehicles. Creaking, human-powered pushcarts jockeyed for space along with diesel-powered trucks belching black fumes. Mostly though, this river was comprised of bicycles: bicycles upon which people rode, sometimes two or three at a time; bicycles beside which others walked, because they were laden with goods; or parked bicycles, leaning this way and that against anything that appeared to be even slightly stationary.

This is my new world, sighed Bill to himself, *so I'd better get into the swim of things.*

Slipping his foot onto the pedal of his own bike, Bill plunged forward into the traffic, taking care not to bump the rear of a cart with its rider perched precariously in front of a cotton bale and unable to be seen from behind.

Just like every other day that week, Bill's focus was on the traffic, the kind of traffic that made his new home feel even more foreign. He had already found a place to lodge, located a few acceptable restaurants, enrolled in the university, and e-mailed some family members and friends back home, but everything still seemed frightfully foreign.

WHAT SHOULD I SAY TO MY FRIEND . . . .

I wonder when I'll start feeling like this place is home, mused Bill, unaware that a single event was about to thrust him into that transformation more rapidly than most.

"Aieeee!" screamed a young man, whose body suddenly was catapulted onto the uneven pavement directly in front of Bill, falling with a sickening thud into a crumpled heap.

Bill abandoned his own bicycle as he raced to the young man's side, fully expecting that others would emerge from the gathering crowd to offer aid. As Bill knelt beside the rider's still form, it was easy to see that the truck, now rumbling off in the distance, had delivered a serious blow, leaving its victim motionless and injured. Bill looked up to ask the crowd for help, but the people had quickly dispersed, almost as if the event never occurred. He was left alone to tend to the young man on the pavement.

A remarkable transformation took place in Bill's heart at the moment he turned to look again at the young man who was now on his knees, struggling to stand. For the first time since his arrival in this strange, crowded city, Bill was no longer looking at masses of people, but at a person, *one single person* in great need.

God, you have put this person into my life for a reason, Bill prayed silently, *and I don't want to blow it. Show me what to do or say so that I can at least leave him with eternity in view.*

"Here, let me help you," Bill urged the young man who was now looking at him with bewilderment. Since he frantically was seeking to gather books and papers from the roadway, it was apparent to Bill that the young man was a university student. "I'll carry your bicycle to the side of the road. Then we can go into that coffee shop and get some water to wash the blood off your head and face," urged Bill, wondering if the young man could even understand his speech. He accompanied his offer with a variety of exaggerated hand gestures, hoping to convey his concern.

"Thank you. Thanks so much," replied the young man, evidently embarrassed by the whole affair. "Really, there's no need for you to help. It was my fault. I have no one to blame but myself. I should have had my mind on the traffic and not on other things. You can go on. Don't let me stop you."

"Nothing doing," Bill protested, surprised that the young man could understand his speech. "At least not until I know you are going to be taken care of properly. Besides, you have no transportation now, so perhaps I can take you where you need to go."

The young man looked surprised. *Who is this?* he wondered. *Why is he caring for me? He looks genuine enough in his concern, but I know he's not from around here.*

"Excuse me," said Bill, almost as if he had read the young man's mind. "My name is Bill. I am a new international student here at the university. I was on my way to classes when you fell on the ground in front of my bicycle. Look, let me buy you some coffee, and we can figure out what to do next."

The young man reluctantly agreed, took out a handkerchief, and began wiping the blood from his face. Bill was relieved to see that the head wound was not serious.

"You're obviously a student," Bill observed. "So where do you attend school?"

"The same as you," the young man replied. "The university. That's where I was headed this morning. Obviously I had something else on my mind—an exam, in fact. And what about you? Tell me about yourself."

"I scarcely know where to begin," Bill replied eagerly. "To be honest, you're the first person I've seriously conversed with since arriving here almost a week ago. I've come here to learn more about your culture and to study the language. Back home, I'm a history major in university, so I thought this would be a good opportunity to broaden my education. I plan to teach, and this experience will look good on my applications—you know, overseas experience and everything. So, what about you?"

"Well," the young man answered, "I grew up in this city, not far from here, and am the first one in my family to attend university. My father would like for me to do what you are doing, study overseas, but I'm afraid that's a long way off. I am still working on the language."

"Language?" Bill exclaimed incredulously. "You seem to have a perfect grasp of the language. I'm the one who's starting at ground zero." Both men laughed as they finished up their coffee.

Bill was encouraged by the openness of his new friend and mentally searched for a way to become better acquainted with him. He especially liked his affable, easygoing manner and his eagerness to learn. Bill needed someone to teach him, and he thought this might be the very person God had sent his way.

"Look," said Bill, "I've missed my class, and perhaps you've missed yours as well. Why don't we order lunch and visit some more? In fact, I have something further to discuss with you, a problem for which you may be the answer."

Over their meal, Bill and the young man reached an agreement. They would each teach the other about his own national history, culture, and language. Both men were excited about the arrangement and even set a date for their first class together.

"You must know," said the young man, "that I am a religious

person. Not as religious as my father or as religious as he'd like me to be. But I *am* a religious person, so we'll have to work around my worship schedule. To be honest, right now I think my god must not like me at all, because I have so many interests. I can't please my own father, so I know I must not be pleasing to my god. I'm even wondering if my accident is some kind of punishment for my lack of enthusiasm about my religion."

"You're not going to believe this," laughed Bill, "but I'm also a religious person. I don't think I'm of the same faith as you, but I still believe very much in God. In fact, a little while ago, I was thanking God that you were not injured seriously. I believe you are an answer to my prayers that He would help me feel at home here and become a good student."

"You were talking to your God just like that?" exclaimed the young man. "I find that impossible to believe. Isn't your God displeased with you all the time? How can you just talk with Him? In my religion, we pray often, but I just as often wonder if my god is listening at all. If he were listening, could he not make me a better person? It's all so confusing. So again, tell me about your God."

Bill looked across the table at his new friend who was, by now, totally oblivious to the wound on his head. He was eager to hear about Bill's God, and Bill was struggling with how best to respond. In spite of his friend's eagerness, Bill thought it would be better to make his response simple, sufficient for the moment. Later, if his friend wanted, they could always discuss the issue at greater lengths.

Bill wondered where he should start the discussion about God. Should he speak of the "omni's" of God's nature: His omnipotence, omnipresence, and omniscience? That would certainly be one way to approach the subject. Perhaps he should deal with the triune nature of God, the fact that He is three distinct and divine Persons, yet one Being. That, of course, would be another approach, although the idea of the Trinity is sometimes difficult to explain to someone of a different faith. Bill didn't want to start out his discussion in a fashion that might end with an argument over the nature of God. Hopefully, there would be time later for that discussion.

Bill's dilemma was not unusual. Grappling with the issue of God's personhood in a brief afternoon discussion is like attempting to take a picture of the Grand Canyon with a throwaway camera. People can get it, but often they just don't "get it." The vastness of God is beyond the human capacity to comprehend totally. That's why the Apostle Paul exclaimed in writing, "Oh, the depth of the riches both of the wisdom and knowledge of God! How unsearchable are His judgments and unfathomable His ways! For who has known the mind of the Lord, or who became His counselor? Or who has first given to Him that it might be paid back to Him again?" (Romans 11:33-35).

Yet, here was Bill's new friend, *asking* Bill about his God and *expecting* an answer. Bill recalled Paul's conclusion to the exclamation above: "For from Him and through Him and to Him are all things. To Him be the glory forever. Amen" (Romans 11:36). He had learned how to unfold that verse and knew that he could give his friend a sufficient, if not complete, answer to his question.

The *reality* of God

"Perhaps I should start with the obvious," said Bill to his inquisitive friend while mentally recalling that Romans 11:36 refers to God four times in three brief statements. "There really is a God, one God, who has revealed Himself to us both naturally and supernaturally."

"I'm not sure I understand what you mean by God revealing Himself to us both naturally and supernaturally," replied Bill's friend, who was by now deep in thought.

"God has revealed Himself naturally through the very order and pattern of the universe which He created," said Bill. "Science, for instance, operates on the basis of this order and pattern, working from what is known and trusted, in order to discover what is unknown. Order, like the earth's revolution around the sun or the 24-hour spin around its own axis, which creates night and day, is the signature of God in the natural realm. That's why it is called *natural revelation*."

"But what about this *supernatural* revelation of God?" Bill's friend inquired.

"This is where things really get exciting," replied Bill, with an obvious degree of heightened emotion. "Years ago, God actually came to this earth physically, in the person of a man named Jesus, who lived among us for 33 years. During the last three years of His life, He publicly displayed His perfect life and miraculous power. He then accepted death by crucifixion at the hands of those who rejected Him. But His death was actually in payment for the sin of all mankind. Three days after His death, He rose from the grave. Then, for several days, He appeared to His followers before ultimately ascending to heaven."

"How do you know this is true?" asked Bill's friend, obviously skeptical.

"There are many proofs," Bill responded, "but one of the clearest proofs is the changed lives of His followers, both then and now.

You can read about this in another supernatural revelation that we call the Bible."

"I've heard of the Bible," said Bill's friend, "but how is it a supernatural revelation of God?"

"Well," Bill said, leaning forward for emphasis, "we should probably discuss this more at another time. But for now, let me just say that over a period of approximately 1,400 years, God inspired at least 40 different men to record His Word to us, so that you and I might know of Him, His love for us, and His eternal plan. The main thing I want to communicate right now is that there really is a God, one God, who is the Sovereign Ruler over all."

Bill's friend sat quietly, seeking to process all he had heard. After waiting for a few minutes, Bill continued, recalling the references to *all things* in Romans 11:36: "For from Him and through Him and to Him are *all things*."

The *realm* of God

"God," said Bill, speaking slowly so the words would sink in, "is the God of the whole universe. He is over *all things* because He created *all things*. All things are *from* Him. He is God over everything that is seen and unseen. He is God over everything that is living and inanimate. He is God over all people, as well as God over all planets. He is God of everything that is outward, to the very limits of space and beyond, and He is God of everything inward, even that which the most powerful microscope can't detect.

"All that God does in His universe, He does well and with perfect integrity. Often we are more concerned with the way things appear outwardly rather than the way they actually are inwardly. God's integrity is revealed by the manner in which He works within the universe. Up on the mountainside where no man will ever walk, there are flowers that are perfect in their blooms. That's God's way of doing things.

"God's way of dealing with mankind is also perfect and …"

"How can you say that?" Bill's friend interrupted. "If God does everything perfectly, how do you explain all the problems people experience, not just here in my own country, but all over the world? You don't have to look around very long to discover that this world is a mess."

"I agree that the world is a mess," laughed Bill. "No question about it. But the problems we have in this world are not the result of failure on God's part but on man's. Since the first man, Adam, chose to sin, this world has been a troubled place to live. What's really remarkable is that it's not in an even bigger mess. Now *that* is a testimony to God's goodness!

"Here's what I'd like for you to remember about God. He is the Sovereign Owner of all things because He created them. And, throughout His realm, God does all things perfectly."

The *reach* of God

Bill was eager to share with his friend the simple fact that God cares for each individual. He wanted his friend to see God's involvement on a personal level. So Bill decided this would be a good place to speak to his friend about three phrases that occur in Romans 11:36: "*from* Him, *through* Him, and *to* Him are all things."

"God is not only *over* all things," said Bill, "His reach, or personal involvement, includes all things. All things have come *from Him*. That means God is the source of all. All things are sustained *through Him*, or through His active involvement in our world and in our lives. In other words, God is the force that holds all things together. And since all of creation is God's, all that happens serves to bring praise to Him.

"The exciting thing about God," Bill continued, "is that He intimately knows you and me and is personally involved in our lives.

"Here's the deal," said Bill as he looked over at his friend. "What concerns you and me concerns God as well. That's why I thanked Him out there on that crowded road. I believe it was God who spared your life and that He did so for a purpose. He has a great plan for your life."

Bill could see that his new friend was struggling to believe in a personal God who actually has a plan for each individual. He knew that in his friend's culture, his god was real but distant, aloof, impersonal, and generally quite angry at humanity. If his friend was like others in his culture, getting his god's attention required vigorous adherence to ritual, accompanied by actions that were sometimes outlandish. A man of his friend's beliefs did not pray because he had his god's attention; he prayed in an exaggerated fashion hoping to *get* his god's attention.

Bill also wanted his friend to know that God's greatest glory was revealed in His accessibility to all who would come to Him in faith. Recalling the exclamation in Romans 11:36, "To Him be the glory forever," Bill spoke to his friend about the praise God justly deserves and will one day receive from all creation.

The *right* of God

"Because God is *over* all things, and because everything is within His infinite reach, He has a *right* to expect that everything, including all created beings, will one day give Him glory. In fact, God will receive glory forever!"

"So, is your God in this for Himself?" asked Bill's friend. "That seems so arrogant and selfish."

"Saying that God has a right to receive glory forever almost sounds selfish or self-centered, doesn't it?" Bill replied. "But remember this, God always does what is best for everyone concerned. Not only does He do what's best for us all, He actually makes Himself available to us.

"In our way of thinking, the more honor a man receives, the more distant and aloof he becomes. It's far easier, I'm sure, for us to get an audience with one of our professors than with the president of the university. The mayor of this city would be much easier for you to contact than the leader of your country.

"God's glory is quite different from man's. It is not indicated by His distance *from* us but by His accessibility to us. You see, God is not only interested in you; He is available to you. In fact, nothing brings Him greater delight than having personal fellowship with His children.

"In Jesus, God became man and lived among us. Now, even though He has ascended on high and is seated at the right hand of God's throne, He also has made it possible for you to have Him within your very heart and seated on the throne of your life. At the end of His earthly life, Jesus, God's Son, died on a cross to pay the price for our sin. Then He was raised up from death to eternal life. Because of that, we may come to God and have fellowship with Him forever. For that reason alone, He should receive our honor, praise, and glory."

"Your idea of God is different from mine," said Bill's friend somberly. "I will have to think about what you have said today. If what you are saying is true, my accident may not have been an accident at all. After all, it *has* brought us together. I want to talk more, but it's late. We must work out a time to meet again. Then we can discuss our history, culture, and language—and maybe even our differing faiths."

Bill's new acquaintance stood, bowed low, and extended his hand in the fashion of a local greeting.

"Welcome to my country, my friend. Soon you must visit my home and meet my family. Now, I can walk home from here, so until another time, good-bye."

"Good-bye, my friend. Good-bye," Bill replied, bowing deeply.

As far as Bill was concerned, this new country was beginning to seem more like home.

Chapter One Review

For from Him and through Him and to Him are all things. To Him be the glory forever. Amen. (ROMANS 11:36)

Early in any serious theological discussion, two issues generally come to the surface: 1) the nature of God and 2) the source and nature of truth. This chapter deals with the first of those issues while the next chapter will deal with the source and nature of truth.

As stated in this chapter, there are many possible approaches when addressing the nature of God. In some settings, it might be more advantageous to speak of God's character, the "omni's" of God. In other settings, a discussion of the triune nature of God might be more fitting. Our goal is to approach each doctrine in a sufficient manner, if not complete, and to base the discussion on a passage of Scripture that can be easily committed to memory. For a brief discussion on the nature of God, it will be helpful to utilize Romans 11:36, a verse in which four issues related to the nature of God are addressed.

What Should I Say to my Friend about God?

The *reality* of God
Natural revelation (PS. 19)
Supernatural revelation (JOHN 1:14; HEB. 1:1-2)

The *realm* of God
God's interest (GEN. 1:1; PS. 139)
God's integrity (JOHN 14:6)

The *reach* of God
From Him (JOHN 1:3)
Through Him (COL. 1:17)
To Him (REV. 22:13)

The *right* of God
Does not demand praise
Deserves praise (ROM. 11:36)

... although He existed in the form of God, did not regard equality with God a thing to be grasped, but emptied Himself, taking the form of a bond-servant, and being made in the likeness of men. Being found in appearance as a man, He humbled Himself by becoming obedient to the point of death, even death on a cross. For this reason also, God highly exalted Him, and bestowed on Him the name which is above every name, so that at the name of Jesus EVERY KNEE WILL BOW, of those who are in heaven and on earth and under the earth, and that every tongue will confess that Jesus Christ is Lord, to the glory of God the Father. (PHILIPPIANS 2:6-11)*

---

*While the accompanying passages above are for the benefit of the student, you may not necessarily choose to use them in an initial discussion with a person who is unfamiliar with the Bible.

What Should I Say to my Friend about the Bible?

Chapter Two

All Scripture is inspired by God and profitable for teaching, for reproof, for correction, for training in righteousness; so that the man of God may be adequate, equipped for every good work. (2 Timothy 3:16-17)

BILL LOOKED ACROSS THE TABLE INTO THE EYES of his friend. Over the past several weeks, those eyes had conveyed warm acceptance, but now they began to narrow in thought, reflecting the difficulty his friend was having with what he'd just been told. For a moment, all that could be heard was the sound of an unfamiliar Eastern ballad emanating from a radio somewhere in the darkened confines of the coffee shop.

"I know you are convinced that what you have told me about God is true," Bill's friend spoke in a subdued tone as he lowered the small cup of coffee from which he'd been sipping, obviously deep in thought. "But I just can't see it. If what you are saying is true, I have believed a lie all my life. What's more, my family and friends also believe the same lie. Why should I accept what you are saying, especially since you are just one voice against many?"

This day had come sooner than Bill had expected. He had been giving his time and energies to establishing a solid friendship with the fellow student he'd first met following the accident on the way to class. They had developed one of those rare, immediate friendships, and Bill soon found himself a frequent guest in his friend's home. Over the weeks, Bill had come to look upon his friend with respect and admiration. Bill often wondered if he'd have been as open if the tables were turned and his friend were an international student enrolled in the university he attended back home.

Bill had not hidden his Christian faith from his friend or his friend's family. They had been eager to share their faith with him as well. Conversations had often lasted well into the night, punctuated with the kind of easy-going laughter so common in an environment where no ultimatums are being issued and where there is an honest, refreshing inquisitiveness. Both Bill and his friend had taken mental note of the obvious differences in their beliefs. Now the time had come for Bill to answer a simple but crucial question: *Where can a man find the truth?*

Those were not the exact words used by Bill's friend. His question had centered more on the issue of authority than truth. "Who has told you these things?" Bill's friend had asked. "And why do you accept them as true?" It was time for Bill to talk with his friend about the Bible.

Bill was ready with the answer to his friend's question and ready to provide his friend with an answer that was both accurate and scripturally based. Bill had learned that the Bible speaks for itself. He had discovered that, in a supernatural fashion, God honors the simple proclamation of His Word.

"I'm glad you asked me about the source of truth," Bill responded excitedly to his friend's question. "This gives me an opportunity to tell you about the Bible, the Book of truth."

Even as he was speaking to his friend, Bill was quietly rehearsing 2 Timothy 3:16-17: "All Scripture is inspired by God and profitable for teaching, for reproof, for correction, for training in righteousness; so that the man of God may be adequate, equipped for every good work." Bill knew that the passage, carefully unfolded, would serve to sufficiently answer his friend's question.

The Bible is *God's* Book

"I want to show you a book," Bill said, taking a small Bible out of his backpack. "This book is God's Book," he continued. "In fact, *all Scripture is inspired by God.*"

"The Bible is God's Book in its entirety," Bill continued, opening his Bible and pointing out that what he held in his hands was in fact a library of 66 books, recorded by 40 men over a period of almost 1,500 years.

"*All Scripture* is inspired by God. Even though many of these men were not acquainted with one another, everything they wrote coincides to give us a remarkable revelation of God and His love and purpose for mankind. In fact, in at least 4,000 different places, you can read that the Bible is the Word of God, all of it!

"The Bible is also God's Book in its essence," Bill stated confidently. "You see all Scripture is *inspired by God*. That means it is literally 'God-breathed.' The Bible is not simply the words of a few men regarding God; it is God's Word to all mankind.

"By the end of the fourth century, these 66 books, divided into the Old and New Testaments, were found to have met the stringent standards required of any writings before it could be assured they were the very Word of God. These standards involved such matters as authorship; exaltation of God and His Son, Jesus, an obviously supernatural character; the condemnation of sin; cohesion (no conflicting statements regarding the nature of God or the person and work of Christ); and the affirmation of the Apostles (men who had actually been with Jesus).

"It *is* true that God breathed His Word through the men who recorded it, and that means that *all* the Bible is inspired as well as *every word* in the original manuscripts. As God's Word passed through the lives of these men, it picked up the 'tint' of their personalities, just as when sunlight passes through stained glass, but it is still God's Word nonetheless. In fact, the earlier portion, which we call the Old Testament, is affirmed as the Word of God over 1,300 times in the 27 books of New Testament."

By this time, Bill could see that his friend was amazed to hear that the Bible was God's Book. His friend knew that if the Bible was truly God's Word, everything written in it carried an awesome degree of authority. It was to be taken seriously and obeyed explicitly. But Bill had even more exciting news to share with his friend.

The Bible is a *good* book

"If the Bible is God's Book," Bill's friend asked inquisitively, "is it possible for me to read it? What is in it for me?"

As his friend posed his questions, Bill mentally reviewed the balance of 2 Timothy 3:16-17, recalling that the Bible is "profitable for teaching, for reproof, for correction, for training in righteousness; so that the man of God may be adequate, equipped for every good work."

Bill's friend sat silently before him, thoughtfully turning the empty cup that now rested on the table, while waiting for Bill's response.

"The Bible is not only God's Book," replied Bill, "it is a good book in every sense of the word. Could I tell you just two ways in which the Bible is a good book?"

With his friend's encouragement, Bill continued. "First of all, the Bible is good in its *approach*, or the manner in which it addresses the important issues of our lives. Let me give you some examples of what I mean by showing you what is contained in the Word of God.

"For instance, the Bible provides us with crucial *teaching*, the important principles to base our lives and faith. In this sense, it is like the architect's blueprint that a contractor follows to build a house. By following the blueprint, the builder knows the result will be similar to what is pictured. God is the great Architect of both the entire world and our lives individually. He wants us to build our lives in a way that is both profitable for us and pleasing to Him, and we can do that by following the principles of the Bible. Building our lives according to His plan will bring us the greatest joy and God the greatest praise.

"The Bible also provides *reproof*, a way that we constantly can test our lives against the standards of God. Think of the builder mentioned earlier. He doesn't just get an idea in mind and start building without caring that the house is level, the walls straight, or the corners square. Instead, a competent builder will carefully prepare the building site, making certain the foundation is both stable and level. Throughout the building process, he will constantly use instruments to check the construction to make sure the walls are straight, level, and square. Likewise, the Word of God reproves our lives, showing whether we are building according to God's plan and warning us when we are not."

"What if we find we're making a mistake and are out of the will of God?" asked Bill's friend. "Then what does the Bible have for us?"

"It happens to us all," Bill responded, nodding his head in agreement, "and God's Word provides *correction*. No one desires that we walk in an upright manner more than God. That's one of the reasons He has given us His Word for *correction*. I have personally found that reading the Word of God on a regular basis helps me to make the kind of corrections I need to walk in a way that pleases God. In other words, God doesn't just show me how I have strayed from His will, He shows me the path I must follow to correct the mistakes I make because of my own sinful carelessness. The Word of God shows me how to stand up straight in my faith."

"It seems that it would be better to simply cooperate with God from the outset," sighed Bill's friend. "That way you could avoid some of the pain that comes from reproof and correction."

"Now you're talking God's language," laughed Bill. "In fact, God's Word provides *training in righteousness*. Since God is the Author of His Word, His Holy Spirit literally takes you by the hand as you read it, showing you the right path. He provides blessing and encouragement as you obey and discipline when you do not. But in a sense, the Holy Spirit, through God's Word, becomes your personal trainer."

"I'm still struggling with what you are saying," said Bill's friend, shaking his head from side to side. It's just so contrary to what I've always believed about God, especially the part about Him caring for me in such a personal manner. I'm especially having difficulty with that."

"Actually, it gets even better!" Bill smiled at the thought of what he was about to share with his friend.

"God's Word is good in its approach, but it's also good in its *aim*, or underlying purpose. You see, God's Word not only shows you how to become a *man of God*; it also provides the instruction you need to face life *adequately, equipped for every good work*. Think of all that's locked up and waiting for you in God's Word. That's why the Bible is said to be *profitable*, or heaped up with instruction and encouragement for every need you'll ever face.

"I can tell I've given you a lot to think about," said Bill, holding up his hands as a signal that he was willing to bring the conversation to a close. "But let me ask you to do something before you discount what I've said. We can talk later if you want, but I'll wait for that invitation. After all, I'm not trying to sell you something.

"My request is simple enough. Here in my backpack I have a small portion out of the Bible called the *Gospel of John*. John was a personal friend of Jesus, so you'll get a first-hand account of what Jesus said and did while He was here on earth. There are 21 chapters in John's Good News, and I'd like you to read one chapter each day for the next 21 days. Then, if you'd like, we can talk. What do you think about my proposal?"

"That doesn't sound too difficult," Bill's friend replied, grinning broadly, "especially since you're not asking me to believe anything, only read. I can do that."

"Then it's agreed," laughed Bill. "I'll wait for your call."

Chapter Two Review

All Scripture is inspired by God and is profitable for teaching, for reproof, for correction, for training in righteousness; so that the man of God may be adequate, equipped for every good work. (2 Timothy 3:16-17)

Inevitably, someone in your geographical, cultural, and linguistic arena will ask you about the Bible. The question may come in many forms, but usually it is about where you find the truth that guides you. For the Christian, there is a simple answer: *God's truth is found in His Word, the Bible.*

But what does your friend need to know about the Bible? If you have memorized the passage above, you will find it easy to give him a sufficient answer.

What Should I Say to my Friend about the Bible?

The Bible is *God's* Book
In its entirety
In its essence

The Bible is a *good* book
In its approach (2 Tim. 3:16-17)
- Teaching
- Reproof
- Correction
- Training in righteousness

In its aim
- That the man of God might be adequate
- Equipped for every good work

Try to master the Bible and soon it will master you!

What Should I Say to my Friend about Man and the Problem of Sin?

Chapter Three

For as in Adam all die, so also in Christ all will be made alive.

(1 Corinthians 15:22)

I*'LL PROBABLY NOT SLEEP AT ALL TONIGHT,* BILL SIGHED as he finished off a second cup of the strong, dark coffee and glanced around the dimly lit room once again to see if he'd accidentally missed seeing his friend. Seeing no one that he recognized, he placed several coins on the table and prepared to leave.

It's just not like him to stand me up like this, Bill thought to himself. Actually, he was both perplexed and irritated. *After all, he's the one who called to say he wanted to visit with me. I wonder if something has happened to him.* That last thought sent a shudder through Bill as he recalled the overwhelmingly anti-Christian sentiment that was so pervasive in the country where he was attending university.

Bill stepped out into the fading light of the evening, unlocked the chain on his bicycle, and pushed it toward the street. Once the traffic cleared, he shrugged to make sure his backpack was secure, threw his leg over the seat, and began to pedal off into the growing darkness. Lights from local businesses began to flicker on as Bill made his way up the street and toward his apartment.

"Bill!" The voice startled him, especially since it was the first he'd heard his name called out in public in the months he'd been away from home. "Bill!" The voice was nearer, and the tone was insistent.

Bill braked and steered his bicycle toward the curb, simultaneously looking over his shoulder to see if he could spot the voice's source. *Maybe I was mistaken*, he thought. But then he heard it again, and this time it was quite near.

"Bill! Wait for me!"

Then he saw his friend's familiar face and eager smile.

"So I was not stood up after all!" Bill grinned as his friend pulled up beside him, out of breath from the chase.

"I'm so sorry!" said his friend. "Please forgive me. My bicycle had a flat tire when I came out to use it, and I had to chase down my brother so I could borrow his instead. He works only a few blocks from my apartment but was making a delivery when I arrived. Anyway, I've caught up with you. Do you still have time to talk?"

"All the time in the world for you, my friend," laughed Bill. "Why don't we go rest over there on that park bench? It looks like a quiet spot for a visit."

By the time they were seated, Bill and his friend had exchanged the usual questions about each other's well being. His friend wanted to get right to the point, however, and wasted no time doing so.

"I have read John's Good News," Bill's friend said matter-of-factly, "and I am not sure what to think about it all. Anyway, I've started reading it a second time. There is so much I don't understand, and I am afraid I have too many questions."

"Probably not!" laughed Bill. "I doubt we'll get to all of them this evening, but let's get started. What did you think about that portion of the Bible?"

"I really like the man, Jesus. He was a truly good man. That is why I am confused as to why some men were so angry with Him, even wanting to see Him die, though He did nothing wrong. I will confess that while reading the first half of the book, I really grew to love Jesus. But He must have done something terribly wrong, something that I do not understand; otherwise, religious people would not have hated Him so. I was also happy to read that He is alive, but I have even more questions about that."

"So what is your *big* question?" Bill asked patiently. "Where would you like to begin?"

"I don't have just one question," Bill's friend replied, shaking his head in bewilderment, "but many questions rolled into one. So let me try to say what is on my heart. If Jesus is God's Son, why did people hate Him so much? If He was God's Son, and He knew they would hate Him, even kill Him, why did He come to earth in the first place? Where does all this hate and evil come from anyway? You tell me!"

Bill looked pensively toward the street where lights were already beckoning the night crowds into local businesses, some of which catered solely to the dark side of human nature. He thought of the first half of 1 Corinthians 15:22, "For as in Adam all die." Turning to his friend, Bill finally spoke.

"Let me tell you a true story, " he said, "and perhaps you will understand why mankind is so filled with sin and why we would all live in punishment forever if Jesus had not come to earth. This story is found in the very first book of God's Word, the Book of Genesis."

Adam was *created*

"Everything around us, whether living or not, was created by God. He created the heavens and the earth. He created all living creatures that inhabit the earth. And finally, God created man. The first man God created was called Adam. And out of a part of Adam's body, God fashioned a companion for him named Eve. Adam and Eve were not just physical creatures like all the other creatures on the earth. They were made in God's image and were alive both physically and spiritually. They walked in harmony with each other and with God. They were really *alive* in every sense. From Adam and Eve comes every human being on earth."

Adam was *commissioned*

"God commissioned Adam and his wife, Eve, to have children and be overseers of the earth. Think of what a wonderful place the earth must have been at that time, especially the Garden of Eden where they lived. Everything, including Adam and Eve, existed in perfect harmony with God. There was no sin or evil in the world at that time."

Adam was *commanded*

"In the place where Adam and Eve lived, God planted a tree called the 'tree of the knowledge of good and evil.' Adam and Eve were presented with an opportunity to show their love for God and their faith in Him by honoring a commandment that He gave to them in respect to this tree. While they could eat of any of the other trees in the Garden, God commanded them not to eat from the tree of the knowledge of good and evil. 'For in the day that you eat from it, you will surely die,' the Lord God said to Adam, who later communicated the same command to Eve."

Adam was *confronted*

"There was a great rebellion in heaven. Lucifer, a magnificent being whose responsibility it was to encircle the throne of God and to reflect His glory, was discontent with his responsibility. Instead of reflecting the glory of God, Lucifer wanted to *be* God. He wanted his own kingdom in which to exercise his wicked rule. As a result of Lucifer's rebellion, God cast him out of heaven, along with one third of the angelic beings in heaven that were under Lucifer's authority. Here, Lucifer would become more commonly referred to as Satan, or the devil.

"Earth, as you recall, was under the dominion of Adam. It became Lucifer's obsession to gain for himself what had been entrusted to Adam. Somehow, he would have to convince Adam to reject the rule of God and accept his will instead. Once Adam bowed to his will, Lucifer would become the 'ruler of this world,' which, as you may recall from reading the Good News of John, was one of Jesus' names for him.

"Disguised as a beautiful serpent, Lucifer *confronted* Adam and Eve in the Garden of Eden, posing a question first to Eve. 'Has God forbidden you to eat from any tree of the Garden?' he asked Eve. 'We may eat of all but one,' replied Eve, 'and that is the tree in the middle of the Garden. God has said we must not eat from it or touch it, or we will die.'

"'You will not die!' responded Satan, who is also called the father of lies. 'God knows that when you eat of that tree, your eyes will be opened and you will be like Him, knowing good and evil.' Eve was attracted to the tree and the fact that its fruit was good for food. She was also attracted by the thought that eating from the tree would make her wise. Deceived by Satan, she took the tree's fruit and ate it. Then Eve gave the fruit to Adam who knowingly and deliberately took the fruit and ate it."

Adam was *cursed*

"The moment Adam and Eve ate the fruit of the tree of the

knowledge of good and evil, they died, just as God had said. But their physical bodies did not die. In fact, they continued to live physically, even bringing children into the world. Neither did they lose their ability to think, express emotions, or make decisions. By all outward appearances, Adam and Eve were very much alive.

"So," asked Bill, seeking to drive home his point, "in what way did Adam and Eve die?"

"I'm not sure that I know how to answer that question," replied Bill's friend. "I see clearly that sin is disobedience to God. And I understand that because of his sin, Adam deserved to pay the penalty just as God had said. But I do not understand how Adam and Eve died."

"Adam and Eve died spiritually," Bill picked up the story again. "They were cut off from God. That's what the Bible means when it says that 'the soul that sins shall die,' or 'the wages of sin is death.' That is not primarily a reference to physical death, but to spiritual death. If a person does die physically without ever resolving the problem of sin, he will be forever separated from God in a place the Bible calls hell.

"God held Adam particularly responsible because he had received and fully understood God's command regarding the tree of the knowledge of good and evil. Adam had clearly acted in deliberate, willful disobedience. Through Adam, sin entered the world, affecting every one of his descendants right up to this very moment. Each one of us as Adam's descendant inherits the nature of sin from Adam. We do not become sinners by sinning; we commit sins because we are already sinners. That's why the Bible says that 'all have sinned and fall short of the glory of God.' Like Adam, we too are under sin's curse. That's what the Bible means when it says that 'as in Adam, all die.'"

Bill took a deep breath and looked into the eyes of his friend. He knew he had been speaking for a long time, but he wanted his friend to hear all of this part of the story, almost without interruption. Bill could tell that his friend was obviously sobered by the thought that all men, even the best, are sinners.

"It all sounds so hopeless," said Bill's friend somberly, looking down at his shoes while remaining deep in thought. "If all of us are sinners, and if sin separates us from God, there is no hope for any of us. We will all end up in that place the Bible calls hell. If you are right, all of these religions, including my own, are just futile attempts to get to God, a God whom we can never reach because of our sin."

"But you have only heard the first half of the story!" exclaimed Bill. "You see, God loves us so much that He has provided a way for the debt of our sin to be paid and for us to have fellowship with Him, now and forever! He even gave Adam and Eve a glimpse of that after they had sinned in the Garden of Eden."

"Then tell me the rest of the story," urged Bill's friend. "But do it quickly. The hour is late, and I must return this bicycle to my brother in just a few minutes. Besides, I have some other errands to run, and I must study for tomorrow's exam."

Bill was suddenly faced with a dilemma. He wanted his friend to experience new life in Christ, desperately so, in fact. But he could tell that his friend was distracted by the necessity of returning his brother's bicycle. Bill was torn as he thought of the fact that this might be his last meeting with his friend. Yet he knew that genuine conversion was always preceded by a conviction of sin so powerful that returning a bicycle would only be a remote thought, quickly dismissed, rather than a driving concern. Bill prayed for wisdom and entrusted his friend to the care of God before speaking.

"It's not the kind of story I want to rush through quickly," replied Bill cautiously, still leaving the door open for his friend to insist on hearing the conclusion of the story. "Besides, I think you can sort some of this out as you read through John's Good News a second time. When you're finished and want to talk, give me a call."

"It won't take me 21 days," laughed Bill's friend as he hopped on the bicycle and pedaled off into the night.

I certainly hope not, said Bill to himself. *I certainly hope not.*

Chapter Three Review

For as in Adam all die, so also in Christ all will be made alive.
(1 CORINTHIANS 15:22)

The problem of sin, and man's inability to resolve that problem successfully, is one of the great issues with which unbelievers wrestle. Wrapped up in the problem of sin are other issues, such as the nature of God, the creation of man, and man's ultimate purpose. A person's awareness of sin and his helplessness in the face of it set the stage for the presentation of the Gospel. The Genesis account of creation and the origin of sin can be used as a key to understanding God's plan of salvation.

The simple outline that follows will enable you to stay on track when telling the story of creation and fall of man. If at all possible, you should proceed with the balance of the story contained in the chapter that follows. In some cases, however, as illustrated in the account of Bill and his friend, it may be necessary to allow an individual more time to think through what you have shared with him. This is often the case in a cross-cultural setting in which concepts must be processed carefully for a full understanding. It is often helpful for a person to consider more thoroughly how the problem of sin can be resolved. The utter helplessness born out of such a consideration, sets the stage for the balance of the Gospel story.

What Should I Say to my Friend about Man and the Problem of Sin?

Adam was *created* (GEN. 1:27)

Adam was *commissioned* (GEN. 1:28)

Adam was *commanded* (GEN. 2:16-17)

Adam was *confronted* (GEN. 3:1-6)

Adam was *cursed* (GEN. 3:7-24)

We do not *become* sinners by committing sins; we commit sins because we *are* sinners.

What Should I Say to my Friend about Jesus, God's Answer for the Sinner?

Chapter Four

For as in Adam all die, so also in Christ will all be made alive.

(1 CORINTHIANS 15:22)

BILL WAS JUST DOZING OFF WHEN THE RING OF his cell phone jarred him awake. He lay in bed for a few moments trying to decide whether he should get up and answer it. Thinking it might be a call from someone back home who, like most of his friends there, was seemingly incapable of calculating the difference in the time zones, Bill swung his feet out of bed and plodded across the floor and into the next room. He was surprised to see that the call was from his friend right there in town.

"I wonder why he's calling so late at night," Bill thought out loud. "Could it be that he's in trouble?" Once again, Bill shuddered at the possibility his friend might have encountered some difficulty because of their open discussions about matters of faith.

Well, I suppose I should return his call. Bill turned on the light beside a chair, sat down, and dialed his friend's number. The voice on the other end was both anxious and excited.

"Bill! Can we talk?"

"Well, sure," replied Bill, still trying to bring himself to a stage of alertness. "What's on your mind?"

"I don't mean talk on the phone," replied his friend. "It's too complicated for that. I mean, can we meet somewhere and talk?"

"That would be fine," said Bill. "What does your schedule look like for the next few days?"

WHAT SHOULD I SAY TO MY FRIEND......................

"I don't mean talk sometime over the next few days. I mean, can we meet someplace tonight and talk?"

"Well," here Bill paused, "do you know what time it is? I'd be happy to meet you, but it's rather late."

"I'm so sorry," Bill's friend groaned apologetically. "Please forgive me. I was totally unaware of the time. It's just that I've finished reading the Good News of John, actually for the third time, and need to know if what I'm thinking is correct. I mean, what I'm thinking about God's answer to the problem of sin. I think it has something to do with Jesus."

"Where would you like to meet?" Bill asked.

"What about the usual place?" his friend responded. "You know, the coffee shop."

"Sure," said Bill, "just give me a few minutes to get dressed, and I'll be right over."

The night air brought Bill fully awake as he walked the several blocks back to the main street market where the coffee shop was located. His friend had found a place back in a quiet corner, and two cups of coffee were already poured and sitting on the table in front of him.

"Thanks, Bill," his friend exclaimed, standing up behind the table and extending his hand. "I'm sorry to get you out like this, but I really do have some questions about John's Good News. You told me to call after I'd read it again. Well, I read it entirely that same night and have now read through it a third time. I hope I haven't bothered you with my call."

Bill thought about the exam he was to take in his university class the next morning, and silently prayed that God would enable him to stay awake through it. *My friend is undergoing an even more*

48   CHAPTER FOUR

important test, he thought to himself, *and I'm the one God has sent to help him prepare for it.*

"So," said Bill, "what's on your mind?"

"I think I've got it figured out, about Jesus, I mean. The last time we talked, I was struggling with the issue of sin, where it came from and why it is so pervasive. You helped me see that everyone has a problem with sin because of the choice Adam made in the Garden of Eden. We have his nature and act the same as he did, deliberately choosing to disobey God.

"But in John's Good News, I've been reading about Jesus. It seems He never sinned, not even when sinful men falsely accused Him and put Him to death. So I think Jesus came to earth to be our example. If we just act as He did, then we will not sin. That way we can have fellowship with God forever. That's the answer, right?"

"Well," Bill replied, "Jesus definitely set the standard for us. He was a perfect example of how we should live. But that's not the primary reason He came to earth. After all, even if you could live a perfect life from this day forward, that wouldn't excuse the fact that you have already sinned. It's inevitable that all men sin. The Bible says that we are all like sheep going astray, each one of us turning to our own way rather than God's. It's not a matter of how much we have sinned or how big we think our sins might have been. That's all subjective anyway. The fact is we are *all* sinners and separated from God."

"Then why did Jesus come to earth if it was not simply to be a good example for us?" Bill's friend had been excited at the thought that he had discovered the truth about Jesus. Now he was perplexed to the point of exasperation.

"Just before we parted the other evening, I mentioned that I had only told you half the story," Bill responded with obvious concern. "Would you like to hear the other half?"

"I have all night," said Bill's friend, "so please tell it to me, all of it. I thought I had solved the mystery of Jesus. Now I'm more confused than ever. And lately I have been thinking more and more about my own sin and wondering if I will spend forever in hell because of it. I have not been sleeping well, so I must have the answer."

You're not the only one who isn't sleeping well, Bill mused silently as he asked the waiter for a second cup of coffee while mentally rehearsing 1 Corinthians 15:22, "For as in Adam all die, so also in Christ will all be made alive."

"While the first part of the story is about Adam, the second part is about Jesus. To fully grasp the role of Jesus, we need to go back to the Garden of Eden," Bill said to his friend who was obviously surprised. "You've heard the bad news of Adam's sin and how it has impacted the life of every person. Now let me tell you some good news.

"As God dealt that day with Adam, Eve, and Satan, He *said* something and then *did* something that proved His love for all mankind, including you. What He said and did indicated His determination to provide a way for man's sin to be paid for by someone other than himself. God made a way for us to be restored to fellowship with Him and to spend forever with Him in a place the Bible calls heaven."

Jesus is *promised*

"First, God *said* something that must have brought delight to Adam and Eve but dismay to Satan. God promised that, one day, a man would be born of a woman who would crush the head of Satan, even though Satan would attempt to destroy that man. That man is Jesus. Perhaps you can recall from reading John's Good News that Jesus sometimes called Himself the *Son of man*. That was His way of reminding Satan that He was the very person God was referring to back in the Garden of Eden."

Jesus is *pictured*

"God also *did* something that showed how Jesus would, one day, pay for the sin of mankind. He performed a sacrifice there in the Garden, shedding the blood of living creatures in order to make garments of skin for Adam and Eve whose sin had now made them ashamed and aware of their nakedness.

"Why do you think God performed a sacrifice?" Bill asked his friend who shook his head and raised his hands, palms open, indicating he had no idea.

"You recall, don't you, that the wages, or payment, for sin is death; not physical death alone, though ultimately every man dies physically, but also spiritual death. That means we are cut off from God because of our sin. Since Adam and Eve were spiritually dead, God moved into the physical arena, showing them a physical illustration of a spiritual principle.

"Blood is the very essence of physical life. In Genesis, we are reminded that the life of the body is in the blood. The blood sacrifice was a picture illustrating that, since the wages of sin is death, the only way our sin could be paid for was by the death of another on our behalf, or in our place.

"God was determined that we not forget the significance of the blood sacrifice. When Adam and Eve's first two sons, Cain and Abel, brought their offerings before God, He accepted Abel's, because it was a blood sacrifice. But God refused Cain's offering, because it was simply an illustration of his own effort to please God.

"Throughout the first section of the Bible, which is called the Old Testament, we read how God moved through history to point the way to that time when the ultimate sacrifice for the sin of the world would take place. When the descendants of Abraham were slaves in Egypt, God raised up a man named Moses to lead them back to their homeland. After Egypt's king repeatedly denied their freedom, Moses warned him that God would move through Egypt, and every home would experience the death of its firstborn.

"God had a different plan for Abraham's descendants. Moses instructed them to gather by families in their homes. They were to sacrifice a lamb and prepare to eat all of it. Prior to the meal, however, the head of each household was to sprinkle the blood of the sacrificed lamb over the top of the door and down each side. When God moved through Egypt that night, He did not bring death to any home where the blood had been applied to the doorpost. The descendants of Abraham were then freed from slavery, a deliverance they continue to celebrate once each year.

"We don't know what animals were sacrificed to make garments for Adam and Eve, but in all likelihood they were lambs. If in the Garden it was a lamb for a man, then in Egypt, it was a lamb for a family. God was clearly moving in history, preparing for the day when, in the fullness of time, the ultimate sacrifice would be made for the sin of the world.

"As Abraham's descendants made their way back to their homeland, God began to instruct them, giving them His laws. The laws of God were a clear standard for behavior, and violation of the laws required specific kinds of sacrifices. It seemed that they were forever standing in line to make sacrifice! And even then, they could not remember all their sins. God responded by giving them another kind of sacrifice.

"The sacrifice made on the Day of Atonement was unique in the sense that it was made on behalf of the entire nation. The high priest would sprinkle the blood of the lamb on a special altar located in a special room entered only once each year to atone for the sins of the nation.

"You can see how God was urging mankind to see the importance of a sacrifice that would be made for the sins of the world. First, in the Garden of Eden, there was a lamb for a man. In Egypt, the sacrifice was a lamb for a family. Then, in the wilderness of Sinai, the sacrifice was of a lamb for a nation. God was preparing mankind for the day when, in the fullness of time, there would be sacrificed a Lamb for the world."

Jesus is *presented*

"Is this making sense?" Bill asked his friend who was now leaning forward, obviously excited.

"It sure is!" exclaimed his friend. "Now I understand something I have read in the Good News of John. When the man named John, the one who later baptized Jesus, first saw Him, he called Him 'the Lamb of God who takes away the sin of the world!' Are you saying that Jesus is the sacrifice for the sins of the world, including mine?"

"You've got it!" exclaimed Bill. "At least you've got part of it. Do you have time for me to tell you the rest of the story?"

"To quote you," replied Bill's friend with a smile, "I've got all the time in the world, my friend."

Bill ordered his third cup of coffee, mentally wrote off the thought of sleep for the night, and plunged into the conversation with renewed enthusiasm.

"Jesus was both the Son of man and the Son of God," said Bill. "The Holy Spirit miraculously conceived Jesus in the womb of Mary, who was a virgin. Because of the manner that Jesus was conceived, He did not inherit the sin nature passed from Adam to all mankind. He did not owe the wages of sin, which is death. But He did die, and His death was on our behalf.

"Think of it like this. Suppose you were arrested for committing a terrible crime and taken to a court where you were to be judged. Now, imagine that I am the judge and that you know me to be an honest and fair man. Since you are a guilty man, it is required that the penalty be fully paid. But what if I stepped off the bench, came to where you were standing, and offered to satisfy the penalty myself?"

"I'd be crazy not to accept your offer," replied Bill's friend, nodding his head in agreement.

Jesus is *put to death*

"That's what Jesus did when He died on the cross. You and I, and all mankind, are sinners. Death, separation from God forever, is the payment for our sin. But as you read in John's Good News, 'God so loved the world, that He gave His only begotten Son, that whoever believes in Him shall not perish, but have eternal life'" (John 3:16).

"I remember those words," said Bill's friend, excited that he could recall so much from his reading. "That's what Jesus said to Nicodemus, who came to Him asking about eternal life."

"Right!" Bill nodded. "When Jesus shed His blood on the cross, He was pouring out His life on our behalf. The Bible says that God 'made Him who knew no sin to be sin on our behalf, so that we might become the righteousness of God in Him.'

"Can you handle a little more?" laughed Bill, "and then we'll go someplace for breakfast."

"I'm waiting," Bill's friend replied, "and then I have a big question I want to ask. Right now, though, you go ahead."

"Well," said Bill, "just before Jesus died, He cried out, 'It is finished!' Many of the people who heard Him would have recognized that statement. You see, often when a man committed a crime, the court would immediately imprison him. On the doorpost of his house, they would sometimes write out the crime and the means of punishment. Then a search would be mounted for someone who was the criminal's next of kin, someone who could make reimbursement for his kinsman's crime. If a near kinsman could be found, and if he agreed to repay for the loss, they would record that repayment on the man's doorpost. When the last payment had been made, they would then write across the doorpost the same words Jesus used, 'It is finished!' That means it is paid in full!

"Now, here's the picture. We are all sinners, imprisoned and bound for death. Across the doorpost of our hearts is written, 'The wages of sin is death.' I can't die for you, or you for me, because we are in jail together. Our only hope is for someone who is, in a sense, our next of kin, someone who is like us in every way except sin. The only person like that is Jesus. That's why just before He died, He cried out, 'It is paid in full!' What we must always remember," said Bill, "is that salvation is an expression of both the mercy and grace of God. God's mercy is evident in that, through salvation, we *do not* have to receive the eternal damnation we justly earned by our sin. God's grace is evident in that we *can* receive something that we could never earn or merit, and that is the forgiveness of sin and eternal life."

Jesus is *proof of eternal life*

"But wasn't He raised from the grave?" asked Bill's friend.

"Exactly!" Bill almost shouted. "Because Jesus was the sinless Son of God, death could not hold Him. If there had been sin in His life, He would have remained in the grave like everyone else who has died. By His death, Jesus paid the penalty for our sin and broke the power of sin and death.

"God raised Jesus up on the third day, just as He had said He would, as proof that sin has been paid for completely. Besides, how could a dead person give you life? The resurrection of Christ is also proof that He lives to give eternal life. People who recognize their sin, turn from it in full repentance, and then turn to Christ in faith, literally receive His resurrected life as their own!

"Do you remember what Jesus said about being born again and how Nicodemus thought He was referring to physical birth? Jesus told him He was not talking about being born again physically but spiritually. You see, when a man is born again, he recovers what Adam lost in the Garden of Eden: fellowship with God and the peace of heart that accompanies that fellowship. 'That which is born of the flesh is flesh,' said Jesus, 'and that which is born of the Spirit is spirit.'

"Whew!" Bill exclaimed, sitting back in his chair and waiting for his friend's response. Bill felt as if a great task had just been completed—and it had!

"I have a question," stated Bill's friend, "but only if you are finished with the story."

What else is there to tell him? Bill asked himself, wondering if he'd left out some crucial part of the story. Thinking of nothing, and weary from the loss of a night's sleep, Bill just shook his head.

"That's all I have to say," Bill replied, "at least for now."

"Then here's my question," said Bill's friend, pursing his lips as he paused to collect his thoughts. "Do you suppose that a person like me could come to Christ and have his sins forgiven?"

With a smile, Bill looked into his friend's earnest gaze, and then toward the window that opened to the street.

Was that the sun rising?

Chapter Four Review

For as in Adam all die, so also in Christ will all be made alive.
(1 Corinthians 15:22)

Ultimately, your friend will ask you about Jesus. The verse above can serve as a ready guide when speaking with your friend about the person and work of Christ. The outline in this chapter, coupled with the outline in the previous chapter, provides a sufficient answer for your friend's most basic questions. Additionally, they provide a means of sharing the Gospel in a non-threatening fashion.

In sharing the material contained in this and the previous chapter, it will be important to remember that you are speaking in the past tense when referring to Adam, "Adam was." In this chapter, however, you are speaking of Jesus in the present tense, "Jesus is."

Remembering the following outline will be helpful in sharing the material contained in this chapter.

What Should I Say to my Friend about Jesus, God's Answer for the Sinner?

Jesus is *promised* (Gen. 3:15)

Jesus is *pictured* (Gen. 3:21; Mal. 4:6)

Jesus is *presented* (John 1:29)

Jesus is *put to death* (John 19:30)

Jesus is *proof of eternal life* (1 Peter 3:18)

For Christ also died for sins once for all, the just for the unjust, so that He might bring us to God, having been put to death in the flesh, but made alive in the spirit. (1 Peter 3:18)

What Should I Say to my Friend about Faith?

Chapter Five

Now faith is the assurance of things hoped for, the conviction of things not seen. For by it the men of old gained approval. (HEBREWS 11:1-2)

"OF COURSE, I NOW BELIEVE EVERYTHING I have read about Jesus in John's Good News. Isn't that what you meant last week when you said that in order to become a child of God, I must repent of sin and receive Him by faith?"

The furrowed brow and anxious tone of the question told Bill that his friend was experiencing a crisis of faith. He was eager to believe in Jesus, desperately so, but he was struggling with the nature of that faith.

"So what does it mean to believe in Jesus, if it is not simply to accept that He is really God's Son, that He came to the earth, lived a perfect life, died on the cross, and rose again on the third day? I accept all those things as true about Jesus, but you seem to be indicating that faith in Jesus is something more than that."

Bill's friend was clearly perplexed. He'd actually been waiting outside a classroom door for Bill's professor to complete his lecture and dismiss the class. It had been frustrating to see Bill approach the professor's desk afterwards and ask him further questions about the lecture that day and the homework assignment, but Bill had finally positioned his backpack a little more securely over his shoulder and walked to the doorway where he was surprised to see his friend.

"May I buy your lunch?" Bill's friend had asked anxiously.

"Sure," Bill had responded. "But there's no need for you to

buy. Let's walk over to the campus cafeteria and see what's on the menu."

Bill could have quoted by heart the never-changing menu. Normally he avoided the cafeteria for that very reason, but the meal together would give him and his friend an opportunity to visit for a while before his next class. They found a table in an out-of-the-way corner and were just getting seated when Bill's friend began to pepper him with questions about what it means to believe in Jesus.

"Allow me to use some verses from elsewhere in the Bible to explain what is meant by faith, or believing in Christ," Bill replied. "I think you will discover that there is a difference in believing the truth *about* someone and believing *in* someone."

The *necessity* of faith

"First, though, I'd like to show you from Scripture how important the whole issue of *faith* really is. Bill pulled his Bible from his backpack and took a small piece of paper from between its pages. The page was wrinkled and somewhat tattered from use.

"These are some areas of our lives in which faith is necessary," Bill continued. "I think you'll find the list interesting."

Across the top of the page were written the words **What Faith Does**. Below the title was a simple list. Each statement on the list was accompanied with a Bible verse.

"Let's start at the top and work downward," said Bill. "I think you'll discover that the issue of *faith* is something God considers really important."

Here is what was on the list:

1. We are **saved** through faith, Ephesians 2:8-9: "For by grace

you have been saved through faith; and that not of yourselves, it is the gift of God; not as a result of works, so that no one may boast."

2. We **live** by faith, Galatians 2:20: "I have been crucified with Christ; and it is no longer I who live, but Christ lives in me; and the life which I now live in the flesh I live by faith in the Son of God, who loved me and gave Himself up for me."

3. We **walk** by faith, 2 Corinthians 5:7: "For we walk by faith, not by sight."

4. We **stand** in faith, 1 Corinthians 16:13: "Be on the alert, stand firm in the faith, act like men, be strong."

5. We **pray** by faith, Matthew 21:22: "And all things you ask in prayer, believing, you will receive."

6. We **overcome obstacles** by faith, Matthew 17:20: " … if you have faith the size of a mustard seed, you will say to this mountain, 'Move from here to there,' and it will move; and nothing will be impossible to you."

7. We **fight** by faith, 1 Timothy 6:12a: "Fight the good fight of faith."

8. We **win** by faith, 1 John 5:4: "For whatever is born of God overcomes the world; and this is the victory that has overcome the world—our faith."

"You see how important *faith* is," Bill was hammering the point home. "In fact, Hebrews 11:6 tells us that 'without faith, it is impossible to please God.' And in Romans 14:23, we read that 'whatever is not from faith is sin.'"

Bill's friend sat back in his chair, still staring down at the sheet that was on the table before him. Bill waited for him to speak.

"I can see that faith *is* very important. But if faith is not simply a matter of believing that Jesus is real and that He did what the Bible says, what is it? Where can I find the answer?"

The *nature* of faith

"I've been hoping you'd ask that question," Bill responded excitedly. "But first let me ask you this question: Where do you think we will find the answer to your questions regarding faith?"

"In the Bible?" responded Bill's friend, more as a statement than as a question.

"Right!" exclaimed Bill. "Remember when we discussed the verses in 2 Timothy 3:16-17? Those verses tell us that the Bible has in it all any man needs to do all things right."

"But I only have the Good News of John," protested Bill's friend, "not the entire Bible."

"I think we might be able to resolve that problem," Bill said smiling, "but for now, I want to show you two verses that tell us what faith *is*."

Bill opened his Bible to Hebrews 11:1-2. Turning his Bible so his friend could follow along, he began to read, "'Now faith is the assurance of things hoped for, the conviction of things not seen. For by it the men of old gained approval.'

"Let's just allow this passage to speak for itself," said Bill. "You will notice that there are three definitions of faith in these two verses.

"First," Bill continued, "we read that *faith is the assurance of things hoped for*. This means that faith is being certain that something you desire is, in fact, a reality, ready for you to claim. Now, not everything you desire is something God wants for you as well. But when your desire is in agreement with God's, He gives you faith.

"How do you suppose God gives you faith?" Bill asked, turning to his friend.

"I have no idea," his friend responded.

"Well," said Bill, "let me remind you of something you have read in the Good News of John. Do you remember anything about the man lying beside the pool of Bethesda who had been ill for 38 years?"

"I sure do," replied Bill's friend, encouraged that he now knew enough of God's Word to participate in a conversation about it. "He was lying beside the pool, unable to walk, hoping someone would help him into the water when the angel of the Lord stirred it. Of course, no one ever helped him."

"Let me ask you some questions about that man," said Bill. "Do you think that the man had ever tried to walk?"

"Sure," replied his friend. "How else would he have known that he couldn't walk?"

"Do you think he wanted to walk?" Bill continued his questioning.

"Of course," his friend responded. "That's why he was at the pool."

"Do you think he really could not walk?"

Bill's friend had to think about that for a moment before answering. "Well, of course he couldn't walk. Any man who doesn't walk for 38 years would find it impossible. His limbs would have withered from lack of use."

Bill pressed the question, "Suppose you asked him if he wanted to walk, and after he responded in the affirmative, you said, 'Well, just get up and walk!' How do you think that man would respond?"

"I think he'd be angry with me. After all, if he *could* walk, he *would* walk!"

"Right," said Bill. "But isn't that just what Jesus did? Didn't He ask him if he wanted to walk? And when he responded affirmatively, didn't Jesus simply tell him to get up and walk?"

"And he got up and walked!" Bill's friend replied.

"Right," Bill responded. "You see, when God's Son, Jesus, spoke to him, faith was born in his heart. Suddenly, he had the assurance that his desire was a reality, ready to be claimed. When God's Spirit reveals to us the will of God, through the Word of God, faith is born in our hearts. We have the assurance that our desire is a reality, waiting to be acted upon."

"I'm beginning to understand," smiled Bill's friend. "But you said there were three definitions of faith in this passage, and that's only one of them."

"The next part of this passage," Bill answered, pointing again to Hebrews 1:1, tells us that faith is *the conviction of things not seen*. In other words, faith is being convinced of the reality of something you cannot perceive with your physical senses. You simply take God at His word and act upon what He says.

"Let me give you an illustration of this statement," said Bill. "Yesterday, I received an e-mail from my father, telling me that he had purchased a warm coat for me, knowing that the winters here can be awfully cold. He told me I could expect to receive it in about three weeks. How do you think I responded to his e-mail?"

"You probably replied by thanking him," Bill's friend responded.

"Right!" replied Bill. "I thanked him for that wonderful coat. Now, I've never seen that coat, felt the leather on that coat, smelled the fur collar, or heard the zipper as it moved up and down the front of the coat. But if you were to ask me if I needed a winter coat, I'd tell you that I have one. Why do you think I am acting so confidently, though the coat is not here with me?"

"I've got it!" Bill's friend fairly shouted. "You have the word of your father!"

"Correct," replied Bill. "And faith is the gift that the Heavenly Father gives us when He speaks to us by His Spirit and through His Word, convincing us that something is real, even though we can't perceive it with our physical senses."

"That's two down and one to go," laughed Bill's friend. "What about this next statement in Hebrews 1:2, saying that by faith *the men of old gained approval*? I don't understand what that means."

"Well, it would help to know a little about these *men of old*," replied Bill. "You see, this is a reference to a great many 'heroes of faith' whose stories are contained in that part of the Bible called the Old Testament. The writer of Hebrews lists them in the verses that follow. You can see their names right here—people like Abel, Enoch, Noah, Abraham, Sarah, Isaac, Jacob, Joseph, and Moses.

"One of these days, I think you will learn the stories of each of the people mentioned in this chapter. But what you need to understand now is that they are each famous for what they *did* in response to what God *said*. This means that faith is not simply something you *think* or *feel*. Faith involves acting on the revealed will of God.

"Their stories remind me of one thing more you should know about faith," Bill continued. "This is something I think you will be able to easily understand. Each of those heroes of faith had to make a very hard choice, a choice as difficult as the one made by the man at the pool of Bethesda! They had to turn from their way, a way

TOM ELLIFF

that seemed so right to them, in order to turn to God and accept His way. That choice to turn is what the Bible calls *repentance*. In a sense, repentance, or turning from sin, is one side of faith. The other side is turning to God. Repenting of sin is more than just admitting sin is wrong; it is turning from sin so that we may fully surrender to the Lord. Sometimes followers of Christ are called *believers*, while at other times they are called *repenters*. Repenting is a necessary aspect of believing. When we turn to Christ as our only Savior and Lord, He enters our lives and brings forgiveness of sin and reconciliation with God. He breaks the power of sin and gives us eternal life."

Bill closed his Bible and looked his friend in the eye. "You see, you might feel that your desire to have forgiveness of sin is a reality ready to be claimed. And, on the basis of God's Word, you might be convinced that something, or someone like Jesus, is real, even though you can't perceive Him with your physical senses. But the ultimate evidence of faith is not what you feel or think. The test of your faith is whether you respond on the basis of what God has said.

"That man at the pool of Bethesda would have remained there until he died, even if he was thoroughly *convinced* that the man standing before him was Jesus and even if he really felt Jesus *could* heal him. His healing came when he responded in faith to what Jesus said to him. He stood up and walked.

"When we first began talking today, you asked if it wasn't enough simply to believe everything you read about Jesus in John's Good News. I know you are convinced that Jesus is real. I think you firmly believe He can save you from the penalty of your sins. What remains is for you to repent of your sin and receive Him by faith, trusting in Him as *your* Lord and *your* Savior."

Bill's friend sat quietly, looking down at his hands that were now folded in his lap.

"Yes," he said, almost inaudibly. "That *is* all that is lacking."

Chapter Five Review

Now faith is the assurance of things hoped for, the conviction of things not seen. For by it the men of old gained approval. (HEBREWS 11:1-2)

Often our excitement over an individual's acceptance of who Jesus is can cloud our thinking and cause a rush to judgment regarding that person's conversion. While it is indeed encouraging when a person comes to grips with the reality of Jesus, we must remember that intellectual assent is *not* the same as faith.

Neither must one's feelings of certainty that Jesus can save be taken as an assurance that he has been saved. The rich young ruler (Matthew 19:16-29, Mark 10:17-30, Luke 10:25-28) is an example of a person who is convinced that Jesus is God and that He has the power to grant eternal life. But in spite of his intellectual assent and emotional assurance that Jesus held the answer to eternal life, he went away from their meeting without trusting in Christ.

At some point, it will be helpful for you to have a discussion with your friend about the nature of genuine faith. At this time, Hebrews 11:1-2 will be helpful.

What Should I Say to my Friend about Faith?

The *necessity* of faith
Through faith
- *Saved* (EPH. 2:8-9)
- *Live* (GAL. 2:20)
- *Walk* (2 COR. 5:7)
- *Stand* (1 COR. 16:13)
- *Pray* (MATT. 21:22)
- *Overcome* (MATT. 17:20)
- *Fight* (1 TIM. 6:12)
- *Gain victory* (1 JOHN 5:4)

Without faith (HEB. 11:6)
Whatever is not faith (ROM. 14:23)

> **The *nature* of faith**
> **Assurance of things hoped** (Heb. 11:1a)
> **Conviction of things not seen** (Heb. 11:1b)
> **Action on the revealed will of God** (Heb. 11:2)

But as many as received Him, to them He gave the right to become children of God, even to those who believe in His name. (John 1:12)

What Should I Say to my Friend about the Church?

Chapter Six

Now to Him who is able to do far more abundantly beyond all that we ask or think, according to the power that works within us, to Him be the glory in the church and in Christ Jesus to all generations forever and ever. Amen. (Ephesians 3:20-21)

BILL WAS EXCITED AS HE MADE HIS WAY TOWARD the city center to meet his friend. *Ecstatic* might have been a better word. He was overjoyed at the openness of his friend and what seemed to be his eager willingness to trust in Christ. From all appearances, it would only be a matter of time before Bill's friend repented of his sin and believed in Christ alone as his Savior.

Perhaps this will be the night my friend trusts Christ, Bill thought to himself as he dismounted from his bicycle in order to cross a major thoroughfare. He was lost in his thoughts as he joined the crowd, moving slowly, shoulder to shoulder, as he made his way across the street.

So how will I go about discipling him? Bill wondered. *Where should I start? We've already spoken about so many things, and he has read the Gospel of John several times.* Bill realized that it was rare for someone like his friend to break ties with his family and his family's deeply engrained religious practices in order to follow Christ. Now that it seemed about to happen, Bill didn't want to make any mistakes.

Bill chained his bike to a light post in front of the familiar coffee shop as the sun was setting. He welcomed the warmth and light of the friendly establishment. The nights had been growing increasingly colder in the past few days, and Bill knew he would soon have to wear warmer clothing. For now, however, a steaming hot cup of dark coffee was just what he needed. Bill found a table off to one side, dropped his backpack beside it, and signaled to the proprietor that his "usual" would be fine. He had grown to love the easygoing hospitality of the country.

When the coffee was placed on the table before him, Bill looked up, rubbed his hands together briskly as he'd seen the locals do, and nodded his head in gratitude.

"Will your friend be joining you as usual?" asked the proprietor, who also served as cook and dishwasher, as well as the only waiter in his own establishment.

"I'm expecting him any minute," Bill replied, "so why don't you bring him his usual as well?"

The proprietor nodded and, smiling broadly, made his way back toward the small room that served as both his kitchen and his home. Bill settled down to collect his thoughts before his friend's arrival.

I want to be ready, thought Bill, *especially if he tells me he'd like to trust in Christ. We'll have a little celebration, but not so much that we attract attention to ourselves.*

Bill had not expected his friend to be late. He was nearly always right on time, if not early, for their meetings. In some ways, his friend's promptness was a unique distinction in a culture that seemed totally oblivious to Bill's Western concept of hours and minutes. Now his delayed arrival was of concern to Bill.

The cell phone in Bill's backpack began to vibrate, and Bill scrambled to retrieve it before the caller hung up. Finally locating the phone, Bill opened it and used the local greeting.

"I cannot come." It was the voice of Bill's friend.

"Oh, no problem," Bill responded. "Do you want to meet somewhere else?"

"I cannot meet you," Bill's friend replied.

"What about later on or even another night? You pick the place and time."

"I'm sorry," replied Bill's friend, "I cannot meet. Not now. Not ever."

"Is there a problem? Are you ill? Are you in some kind of difficulty? Do you need me to come to you?" Bill was almost frantic.

"It is not your problem. I cannot meet with you. I am sorry, but I cannot come. Good-bye."

Bill's hand was trembling as he lowered the phone to the table, repeating to himself the conversation that had just taken place. His earlier exuberance was now melting like an ice cube in the sun. Something had gone terribly wrong, and Bill had not the slightest clue what had happened.

"More coffee?" This time the waiter's eyes and mannerisms seemed strangely knowing, as if he'd been aware of Bill's interests and of the nature of the phone call. A chill ran down Bill's spine, and for the first time he felt out of place.

Bill shuddered uncomfortably, placed his money on the table, and left abruptly. The outside air had a biting chill that did nothing to diminish the feeling that he was a foreigner and that this was not his home. Bill quickly unlocked his bicycle and headed back to his apartment. Even in the familiar surroundings of the apartment, Bill suddenly became acutely aware of the traffic noise on the street below and the strange smells wafting over from the restaurant next door.

I don't like it here, Bill thought to himself. *Maybe it's all a mistake. Perhaps I should just withdraw from the university and return home.*

Bill first sat on the edge of his bed, attempting to sort out a confusing wave of emotions that had caught him off guard. He then abruptly fell to his knees beside his bed and began to pray.

"Father, is this fear?" Bill questioned aloud. "Homesickness? Anger? Suspicion? Am I just disappointed and disillusioned? Depressed, because my hopes have been dashed? Concerned for my physical safety? What is happening to me? I confess that I have never felt so alone—and so 'foreign.' I would really love to speak with someone from home, but right now, I'm so glad that I can speak with You."

At first, as Bill prayed aloud, he thought he was mistaken about hearing the sound of his cell phone, vibrating in the backpack he'd dropped just inside the apartment door. For a brief moment he ceased praying, just to make certain. There it was again. It *was* his cell phone. Bill moved quickly across the small room, almost crawling, in an attempt to retrieve the phone before the caller hung up.

"Uh—Hello!" Bill said, just on the edge of being out of breath.

"Bill?" asked the caller. "Bill, is that you? Can you hear me?"

"I've got you!" replied Bill, sorry that he hadn't checked the caller ID first to see who was calling. "Who's this?"

"It's me, Chris—Chris Foster. How are you, buddy? Hope I didn't get you out of bed."

"Chris?" Bill exclaimed. "You gotta be kidding! I was just …"

"Like I said," Chris butted in, ignoring the long distance delay, "I sure hope I didn't get you out of bed. Of course, you got *me* up and out of bed, so I had to call."

"What do you mean?" asked Bill. "You know, about getting out of bed. I'm still awake, but how did I awaken you?"

"I really don't know," laughed Chris. "Of course it's early morning over here, and I just suddenly woke up, wondering if you were in some kind of a problem. I thought maybe some spiritual warfare might be going on in your life, or at least you were experiencing some kind of difficulty. I know it sounds crazy, but *you* woke *me* up, and I had to call!"

"Chris, it's not crazy at all," Bill responded. "You got time to talk a little?"

"All the time in the world for you, my friend."

Bill recalled when he'd first heard that statement from his friend and former student pastor, Chris Foster. Bill's car was in the shop, and he was asking around church for a ride to school the next morning. Chris had overheard and volunteered to pick him up. On the way to school the next morning, Bill had opened up to Chris about his questions regarding his relationship with God.

"Look," Bill had said, "I don't have class for another hour. Do you have time to talk?"

"All the time in the world for you, my friend," Chris replied, using a phrase that Bill not only often heard from Chris over the next few years, but one he'd grown accustomed to using himself.

Right now, Bill could not have been more encouraged to hear from anyone else. Chris had been both a friend and a mentor. In fact, Chris had been the one who'd later encouraged Bill to consider this "overseas adventure with a purpose," as he'd called it.

"Chris, I've got a real problem—and you may be right, by the way. It could just be a matter of spiritual warfare." Bill knew that Chris would shoot straight with him. Chris didn't have a lot of mercy, and he didn't beat around the bush when dealing with a problem. He always went straight for the jugular.

"Tell me about it," urged Chris, "but try to finish before your battery does." Chris was aware of Bill's penchant for long conversations, the kind that sometimes tried a friend's patience, and he had no trouble chiding Bill when the talk began to stretch out.

"Once I've got the story straight, I'll tell prayer warriors of the church," Chris continued, "and we'll go to work on it from our end."

"I'm not sure there's much that can be done on that end," replied Bill dejectedly. "The problem's over here, and I don't know what to do about it." Bill poured out the story of the past several months, beginning with his "chance" meeting and newfound friendship. Hitting the high spots of his friend's growing interest and apparent willingness to trust Christ, Bill ended by telling of the confusing call earlier in the evening.

"That's when this emotional tsunami hit me," said Bill. "And that's why I said the problem is here, and there's not anything my church friends back home can do about it."

"You know, Bill," laughed Chris, "sometimes I wonder if you ever listened to anything I taught you. Obviously you have forgotten the study I conducted last summer with our campus group. It sure seemed to me like you were awake, especially with all your questions. But then maybe you were just in a trance."

"I'm sorry, Chris," replied Bill, "but I'm a little rattled right now, so refresh my memory. I'm listening. Promise! I'd like to know how my church fits into all this. If you've got the answer, have at it. I've got all the time in the world for you, my friend." Bill scooted over to the wall, plugged the battery charger into his phone, and leaned back against his bed.

"I can't go into all the details," Chris began, "so first let me ask if you have any notes in your Bible from that study in the book of Ephesians. Anyway, grab your Bible and let's take a look at what God says about the church, and why you really need your church right now."

"Hang on for a second," said Bill excitedly, once again reaching into his backpack, this time for his Bible. "Got it! So let's go!"

"As you *should* have recalled," said Chris, tongue in cheek, "we noted that, in its most simple expression, the church is a self-governing, local fellowship of believers who have openly expressed their faith through the symbol of baptism. Our understanding of the church and its practices expands as we trace its development throughout the New Testament. Each passage gives us added insight, so we want to consider the whole counsel of God's Word. For now, I want us to look at the concept of the church as Paul describes it in Ephesians."

"I've got my Bible open to Ephesians," said Bill, "and can actually read a few of the things I have written in the margins. I wish I had my full set of notes."

"Not a problem," replied Chris. "I'll not be going into detail, but I do want you to see some pictures of the church. That way you'll understand how important the church is to your ministry there. Hopefully, you'll someday be able to locate some other believers there in your community. But until then, we're the best you've got, so we want to do our job well.

"In his letter to the church at Ephesus," Chris continued, "Paul used some word pictures to help us understand the church and its role in our lives. He refers to the church as:

1) **The brothers of Christ**—sons of God who share in His inheritance (1:1-14)

2) **The building of God**—built with Christ Jesus Himself as cornerstone (2:19-22)

3) **The body of Christ**—with Christ as head (1:22-23, 4:15-16)

4) **The bride of Christ**—for whom He gave His very life (5:25-32)

These word pictures help us see the significance of the church."

"I've found where I've written each of those word pictures out beside the Scriptures you mentioned," said Bill. "I must have been at least partially awake while you were teaching. But I still don't see what that has to do with your call and how the church there has a responsibility for me here."

"Well, hold on for a minute and I'll get there," laughed Chris. "It's obvious that you haven't lost that inquisitive nature for which you're so famous. Let me press on a little more."

The *brothers* of Christ

"First, Paul reminded the believers in Ephesus that they were *brothers*," continued Chris. "In that passage, he speaks of the fact that they have been adopted into God's family. Elsewhere in the Bible, we read that through the miracle of the second birth, we are born into God's family. In just a minute, we'll see that we are also in God's family by virtue of our 'marriage' to Christ.

"Here's the point, Bill—you and I are brothers, we're in the same family of God, and that places a heavy responsibility on us both. When I was awakened a few minutes ago by the thought that you might be experiencing some sort of difficulty, I knew I had a responsibility. I knew it was important for me to talk to the Father about you. I probably didn't need to call you so late in the evening, but I wanted to know how to pray for you. A missionary in China, Rosiland Goforth, once wrote a short poem that has had a dramatic impact on my life.

> *I cannot tell why there should come to me*
> *A thought of someone miles and years away,*
> *In swift insistence on the memory,*
> *Unless there is a need that I should pray.*
> *We are too busy to spare thought*
> *For days together of some friends away;*
> *Perhaps God does it for us—and we ought*
> *To read His signal as a sign to pray.*
> *Perhaps just then my friend has fiercer fight,*
> *A more appalling weakness, a decay*
> *Of courage, darkness, some lost sense of right;*
> *And so, in case he needs my prayers—I pray.*[1]

Anyway, Bill, you're my brother. All of us here, as part of your family, will be talking to the Father on your behalf."

"That's a sobering thought," replied Bill, in a voice that was equally subdued.

The *building* of Christ

"There's even more," Chris continued. "Paul reminded those members of the church in Ephesus that they were also God's *building*, built on the foundation of the apostles and prophets with Christ as the cornerstone.

---

[1] Goforth, Rosiland. *How I Know God Answers Prayers*. 3rd ed., (Nappanee, IN: Evangel Publishing House, 2001), p. 20. Used with permission, Evangel Publishing House.

"That's a great picture! Here you have two parts of one foundation: the Old Testament built upon the prophets and the New Testament built upon the apostles. But notice that these two load-bearing foundations are joined together at the corner by Christ, the cornerstone. In Paul's day, the cornerstone was the first stone to be laid. It would tie the load-bearing walls together and serve as a point of reference for the entire building."

"What a great picture of Jesus!" exclaimed Bill. "He is the One who ties together both the Old and New Testaments. But I have to ask you again, what does this have to do with me and the church?"

"You're part of God's building, aren't you?" asked Chris. He continued because the answer was an obvious "yes." "What would you do if you saw that part of the structure in which you are now living had become seriously weakened?"

"I'd go to the manager," replied Bill.

"And that's exactly what I did when I awoke a few minutes ago with a burden for your welfare. I talked with the 'Manager' before I called you."

"I'm beginning to get the picture," said Bill, "and I'm really encouraged by what you are saying. Frankly, the idea of my church being so concerned for me is something I'd never really thought of before. I've just considered myself as God's 'Lone Ranger.'"

"Not at all," said Chris. "In fact, a group of us were praying for you just yesterday."

"Wow!" exclaimed Bill. "So how does the 'bride of Christ' fit into the picture?"

The *bride* of Christ

"That's especially exciting," Chris answered. "Marriage is a covenant relationship. Back in Bible days when a covenant was struck between two people, they would often seal it by cutting an animal in half, nose to tail, then walking between the two pieces. The Old Testament word translated 'covenant' has in it a sense of 'cutting.' Finally, they would stand together between the two pieces of the animal and exchange tokens of the covenant. Exchanging coats meant 'my identity is yours and yours is mine.' Similarly, the exchange of belts signified shared strength. And the exchange of swords signified that they would mutually stand against their enemy. Looking at the pieces of the slaughtered animal, they would then agree that God should do the same if either broke the covenant.

"Of course, we don't follow that practice at weddings, thank the Lord, but there is an exchange of tokens, or rings, to symbolize that the bride and groom are entering into a covenant between themselves and the Lord. Once they are pronounced husband and wife, they are welcomed by each other's parents on the basis of a new relationship with their child.

"Throughout the Bible, the Lord is referred to as the Bridegroom and His people are called the *bride*. This is especially true in the New Testament. In essence, an exchange of vows took place at your conversion. You said, 'I do,' to Jesus, and He said, 'I do,' to you. God the Father then said, 'Welcome home. You are accepted in the Beloved, My Son, Jesus.'

"In Ephesians 5:25-32, we read of Christ's loving concern for the welfare of His bride. So I'm not the least bit surprised that He's prompted someone to check on you today."

"Incredible!" gasped Bill. Chris could not see him, but Bill was shaking his head from side to side in amazement. "And what about the church as the body of Christ?" Bill insisted. "There's bound to be a lesson for me in that as well."

The *body* of Christ

"To me, that is the very best picture of all," answered Chris. "We are the *body* of Christ, indwelt by the Holy Spirit, each equipped with God-given abilities for service, which Paul, in Ephesians 4:11-13, refers to as spiritual gifts. And the passage in Ephesians 4 is just a short list! In the New Testament we read of at least 19 different spiritual gifts.

"Elsewhere, Paul reminds us that we each possess different gifts for a very important reason. Like the various appendages of your physical body, each performing a specific work, the exercise of spiritual gifts allows those around us to receive the ministry of Christ, just as if He were right here in His physical body. That's why the church, as Christ's bride, is also the body of Christ.

"Apparently, my particular spiritual gift involves exhortation," said Chris, "because when I was making this call, I prayed that the Lord would show me how to both encourage you and show you how to resolve whatever problems you are facing."

"That *is* encouraging," replied Bill. "So it's really not just me and God over here. I've got a whole group of friends in my church back home who have been summoned by God and equipped to minister to me in time of need."

"Listen, Bill," said Chris Foster, with an urgent tone in his voice, "my phone's beeping, which means my battery is about dead. Anyway, my billfold has been drained, I'm sure. So let me pray with you and then ..."

The hissing silence told Bill that Chris's phone had indeed gone dead. Strangely, the earlier feelings of fear, disappointment, and discouragement were gone, as was the overwhelming sense of loneliness. Bill stood up and began to gather up his backpack and Bible that were lying on the floor. As he reached to pull the plug of his battery charger from the wall, his cell phone vibrated once again.

It's probably Chris, just wanting to sign off, Bill thought, this time checking the caller ID. He was brought to an immediate sense of alertness by what he saw. It was his friend all right, but not his friend, Chris. This time, the call was from his student friend in the city.

"Hello, this is Bill," he said, silently praying the call was not a sign of trouble.

"Bill, it's me!" his friend whispered. "I must apologize for my earlier call. There has been some trouble. My father and brothers have been questioning me about our meetings, and I have told them the things you have been telling me. My father is very sad. I have never seen him so sad since his mother died. My older brothers are angry. They wanted to come take you from the restaurant this evening. My younger brother is quite interested in what we have been discussing, which makes my older brothers even angrier. Anyway, that is why I could not come see you this evening. In fact, they have forbidden me to meet with you again."

Bill's heart broke at the thought that his well-intended discussions had now placed his friend's life in danger, and his own as well. He grasped for words to convey his concern and fumbled in the attempt.

"I … I am so sorry," Bill said, at once seeking to control his grief and fear. "What should I do? What can I do? Do you need a place to come for safety?"

"No ... no ... please. Everything is fine now," Bill's friend replied. "In fact, my father has gone to sleep, and my brothers and I have talked until we are all weary. I told them that you were simply answering the questions I had brought to you and that I had been telling you about our faith as well. They are not angry now.

"But I do have a problem, and you must help me."

"And your problem is ..."

"I am troubled by what you are sharing with me. I believe you are speaking the truth of God. From tonight, I know I must continue to pursue the path of faith in Christ. But there are huge consequences if I do so. At the most, it could mean my life. At the least, I will be cast out from my family. I know I must make the right decision and wanted to talk with you about it."

"I've already asked the church to pray for you," said Bill, grimacing at his insertion of a term he'd yet to share with his friend.

"Church?" asked his friend. "What is church? How can they pray for me?"

"Well," replied Bill, silently praying for the right words, "there are some people who care very much about you. They are praying to God for you, even today. It would take too long to tell you about the church. Besides, we may never have the opportunity to speak again, and there are other things to discuss."

"But, Bill," his friend interrupted, "I must know about this church and the people who are praying for me. Don't you have time to tell me about it now?"

Bill smiled as he sat back down on the floor and plugged the battery charger into the wall.

"I have all the time in the world for you, my friend, all the time in the world."

Chapter Six Review

Now to Him who is able to do far more abundantly beyond all that we ask or think, according to the power that works within us, to Him be the glory in the church and in Christ Jesus to all generations forever and ever. Amen.

(EPHESIANS 3:20-21)

There is so much to be said regarding the doctrine of the church that using only a single verse would be a disservice. In this instance, when asked about the church, I have found it easier to recall four word pictures found throughout the book of Ephesians. You will note that the emphasis of this chapter has not been so much on the mission, or the practices of the church, as it has been on the church's nature.

When asked about the church, you may choose to do as the Apostle Paul and speak of it using the following analogies:

> ## What Should I Say to my Friend about the Church?
> The *brothers* of Christ (EPH. 1:1-14)
>
> The *building* of God (EPH. 2:19-22)
>
> The *body* of Christ (EPH. 1:22-23, 4:15-16)
>
> The *bride* of Christ (EPH. 5:25-32)

And He [God] put all things in subjection under His feet, and gave Him [Jesus] as head over all things to the church, which is His body, the fullness of Him who fills all in all. (EPHESIANS 1:22-23)

What Should I Say to my Friend about Baptism and the Lord's Supper?

Chapter Seven

And Jesus came up and spoke to them, saying, 'All authority has been given to Me in heaven and on earth. Go therefore and make disciples of all the nations, baptizing them in the name of the Father and the Son and the Holy Spirit, teaching them to observe all that I commanded you; and lo, I am with you always, even to the end of the age.'

(MATTHEW 28:18-20)

BILL'S HEART WAS HEAVY AS HE WALKED ACROSS the campus. Weeks had passed with no contact from his friend. In a sense, the burden for his friend had become a blessing to Bill. He no longer spent time reflecting on cultural differences or linguistic barriers. He wasted no time thinking of things he liked or disliked about his environment. In fact, he no longer thought of the country as his "new" home. A consuming sense of *mission* had replaced the feelings of *foreignness*.

Bill was on a mission. He desperately longed to see his friend come to Christ. But for the present, all he could do was pray and cautiously solicit the prayers of his church back home. Bill had quietly sought to find a believing community on the university campus, but so far nothing had surfaced. In a strange way, he felt a greater necessity for the support of his church than he'd ever felt before. *They are in this with me*, Bill had concluded, *and some day, by God's grace, I believe we will see a positive change in my friend's life.*

Bill found his bicycle right where he'd left it that morning. He determined to eat early and spend the rest of the evening studying for the next day's exam. First, however, he decided to make his daily

WHAT SHOULD I SAY TO MY FRIEND..........................

visit to the post office, hoping that perhaps a new CD of his church's praise service might be discreetly placed in a package from home.

Originally, it was not planned for Bill to be alone on this adventure as a student in a foreign university; a "student with a purpose" was the way he had explained it to his church family. His fellow team member from back home had run into visa problems, however, and now that the semester was almost over, it appeared he would not be coming at all. Bill found occasional comfort and encouragement in listening to his church's worship services on the Internet. He loved his pastor, and his veiled references in his messages regarding Bill really picked up his spirits, although he'd later sent a word of caution to his well-meaning pastor.

Bill also loved to worship through music. Sometimes he'd even lose track of time as he lay on the floor of his apartment, listening to the Word as it was preached and sung. Where he'd once had a daily "quiet time" as a matter of discipline, it was now desperation that drove him. He had concluded that his tough times were actually good for him.

Sometimes Bill even wondered what forms genuine worship would take in this strange setting as Christ began to grow His church here. *I'm sure He has that worked out!* Bill laughed to himself, reminded that, one day, a multitude from every tribe, tongue, and nation would surround the throne of God, singing His praises.

On the way to his apartment after going by the post office, Bill passed the coffee shop where he'd last met with his friend. *I'll just go in and grab a bite before heading home*, he said to himself on an impulse. Parking his bicycle, he slung his backpack over one shoulder and walked through the door into the darkened room.

"Hello, my friend! Where have you been? I haven't seen you in weeks!" It was the restaurant's proprietor. In spite of his warm greeting, Bill still remembered their last conversation, and the suspicions he'd set aside rose again in his heart as the hair stood up on the back of his neck.

"I suppose you'll want the usual," the proprietor continued, showing a row of yellowing teeth as he smiled broadly.

Bill nodded as he dropped his backpack into the chair beside a table near the door.

"Why don't you take another table?" urged the proprietor, motioning with his head toward the back of the room.

"Uh, sure," Bill replied, lifting his backpack and looking toward the back of the restaurant for an empty table. His eyes, now adjusting to the darkness, scanned the room for an empty table to the rear. For a moment, he thought he'd seen a familiar face but assumed his mind was playing tricks on him. Looking again, however, he saw that his assumption was a reality. There was his friend, standing to his feet, smiling and waving him back to the table.

"You have finally come!" exclaimed his friend. Moving from behind the table, he brushed Bill's outstretched hand aside and embraced him warmly. "Sit down, please! We must talk! This is an answer to my prayer!"

"What do you mean?" Bill asked, still attempting to sort through what this chance meeting would mean.

"I have come here every day for the last two weeks," his friend replied excitedly, "hoping to find you. A few moments ago, I prayed, 'God, if you really want me to continue my journey to Christ, bring my friend to meet me.' I had decided that if you did not come today, perhaps God did not want me to trouble myself any longer.

"But see, you are here, my friend!" Bill's friend could scarcely contain his excitement.

"But what about your family?" asked Bill, wondering if his friend's life was at risk for meeting with him.

"My father has said that I am of the age to make my own choices in life and that it would be impossible for him to stop me from searching. He said that he had once had such questions but laid them aside when his friends began teasing him.

"My elder brothers have said I must not discuss the matter when I am at home, because it only brings trouble to the house. They are actually not so religious, as you know, and always enjoyed speaking with you. As my eldest brother said, their lives are already difficult enough without making more trouble. Since my eldest brother is the one with the money and the one who paid for my cell phone, I returned it at his request.

"My younger brother has asked repeatedly if we could talk further about the matter since he, too, has questions. I have wanted to honor my father and not trouble my older brothers, so we have not discussed it any longer. Now I feel the time has come to obey God rather than man.

"I have continued to read John's Good News, five more times, in fact," Bill's friend continued excitedly. "Two weeks ago, I saw that I was no different than all those people who hated Christ, even the ones who put Him to death. I wanted to come to God, but my sin was a barrier between us. I begged God to show me the way. That night, Jesus came to me in a dream, saying, 'I am the way, the truth, and the life.' When I awoke, I knew that I had read those words in John's Gospel. I found them and read Jesus' words that no one could come to the Father except through Him.

"I prayed, 'Father, I don't know all that you mean by this, but I am coming.' So I have been waiting here each day for you to tell me how I may come to God."

Though he had been praying for this moment, Bill was stunned at his friend's request. He lowered his eyes, looking down at the table in an attempt to conceal the tears that were now filling them.

"So you are convinced that you are a sinner and have no power to come to God?"

"That was the issue that troubled me the most," answered his friend. "All my life, I have believed that the only way any man could come to God was through his good works. I saw in John's Good News that some very religious men, men who kept God's laws, were still sinners and away from God. I knew I was not as good as those men, so I am certain I cannot come to God on my own. In fact, I believe what Jesus said about no man coming to the Father except through Him."

"But what about Jesus' death and resurrection?" Bill continued to probe.

"It is as you told me," his friend replied. "He died as full payment for my sin and is risen so that He might give me eternal life. That is the life I must have, Bill, and you must tell me how to receive it."

Bill looked down at his hands, thinking hard about what he should say next to his friend. Looking up into his friend's eyes, he continued.

"You have read John's Good News and how he said that 'as many as received Him, to them He gave the right to become children of God, even to those who believe in His name, who were born, not of blood nor of the will of the flesh nor of the will of man, but of God.'"

"I have read that!" Bill's friend interrupted, "and that is what I am doing. I am repenting of my sin and, by faith, acknowledging Christ as my Savior and my Lord. I am choosing to believe in Him!"

"Then what does the Word of God say is true of you?" Bill asked slowly, emphasizing each word.

"It says that ..." His friend's eyes grew wide with excitement. "It says that I *am* a child of God!"

Slapping both hands on the table, palms down, Bill's friend exclaimed, "Can it really be true?"

"You tell me," replied Bill, grinning from ear to ear.

"It *is* true," he replied. "I am now a child of God!"

The two men sat in the coffee shop for hours, talking into the early evening with no thought of the next day's exams. Bill was surprised at how much he remembered of what Chris Foster had taught him, especially in those early months after Bill had come to Christ.

Bill was especially concerned that his friend understand the eternal nature of his experience with Christ. Coming from a culture and faith system in which reward was based entirely on human effort and blamelessness, Bill's friend needed the assurance that this new life he was experiencing would endure, regardless. Almost without thinking, Bill launched into a subject that took their conversation in a totally different direction.

"You see," said Bill, "the new life that you are experiencing is the resurrected and eternal life of Christ Himself. When you are baptized, that is a picture of the 'old you' identifying with Christ's death on the cross as payment for your sin. When you are raised up from the water, that is a picture of your identification with Christ's resurrection into eternal life, the new life you now possess since you have trusted in Him."

"Baptized?" queried Bill's friend nervously. "I remember reading in John's Good News about John the Baptizer who baptized Jesus. I also remember something else about the questions Jesus' followers had concerning John's baptisms. But to be honest, I haven't given that any thought. If I did not receive my eternal life because of something I have done, why is it important for me to be baptized? I'm not opposed to doing what I should, but I guess I just don't understand."

"You've asked a really good question," Bill replied, "so I want to be careful how I answer. Let me explain what the Bible teaches about baptism and another practice we often call the Lord's Supper."

Bill looked at his watch and thought about his studies for the next day's exams. Looking back up at his friend, he asked, "Do you want me to explain about baptism and the Lord's Supper right now? What I mean is, do you have time?"

"All the time in the world for you, my friend," Bill's friend grinned mischievously.

"You're a fast learner!" Bill laughed, reaching down for the Bible in his backpack. Laying his Bible on the table, Bill began his explanation of the two ordinances of the church, baptism and the Lord's Supper.

"It's important for you to know that the foundation for all our beliefs and practices is found in God's Word. Four of the 66 books in the Bible tell us about the ministry of Christ while He was here on earth."

"I suppose John's Good News is one of those books," said Bill's friend.

"Correct," affirmed Bill, "and the others are the Good News according to Matthew, Mark, and Luke. But there are still other books that tell us what happened after Jesus completed His earthly ministry and ascended to heaven. Those books tell us about the early growth and expansion of Christianity, how the church was organized, and what those early Christians believed and practiced. It is from this record that we have guidelines for our beliefs and practices, right up to this very day.

"Throughout the Bible, we read how important it is to remember significant events that have occurred in our relationship with God. God wants us to recall these events with a good understanding of what happened and with gratitude in our hearts for His grace and mercy. God is especially concerned that we understand the full significance of our salvation and the fact that our salvation required the death of Jesus on the cross. To aid our memory, He has given us two pictures, or ordinances: baptism and the Lord's Supper. While participation in these two ordinances does not save us, it does present an outward expression of an inward reality.

"Baptism, or immersion, is a picture of what happened in one's life as he believed in Christ and was born again into eternal life. The Lord's Supper is a continuing reminder that Jesus made salvation possible by His death and that He will one day return for all who follow Him. We practice these two ordinances because of Christ's command to do so and because we see in the Bible that this was the practice of the early church."

"But what role does the church play in all this?" asked Bill's friend. "After all, isn't my salvation a personal matter?"

"Of course your salvation is a personal matter, strictly between you and God. In Baptism and the Lord's Supper, we give open testimony to our union with Christ, recount His death, and rejoice in His imminent return. That is why we observe them with believers of similar faith and practice. We place ourselves in a position of accountability within a local church so that we might mature in our faith. This helps us in our spiritual journey and gives the world a clear expression of Christ's love as they see His lordship over our lives."

"But I've never seen either of these ordinances or even a church," protested Bill's friend, "so how can I be baptized and have the Lord's Supper?"

"Before I was baptized," Bill replied, "I sat in a class with some other new believers and learned the importance of what I was about to do. I was very serious about my Christian faith, so I took careful notes and later copied them here in the back of my Bible."

Bill turned to the back of his Bible and removed a small folded paper.

"Here," Bill said. "Perhaps it would be best for us to look at these notes together." Turning his chair so that he and his friend could look at it together, he began to read the following, stopping periodically to answer his friend's many questions.

When is an Ordinance Properly Administered?

USING SCRIPTURE AS A GUIDE, we find that the ordinances of baptism and the Lord's Supper are properly observed when five issues are satisfactorily addressed:

1 **The proper candidate:** For baptism, this is someone who has *already* experienced the grace of God for salvation and now desires to make that a matter of open confession (See Acts 8:36-38, 10:47-48). For the Lord's Supper, the proper candidate is someone who has been saved and has made a public confession of that fact through baptism. It should also be a person who is in fellowship with his local church and whose personal spiritual life is consistent with that portrayed in Scripture (See 1 Corinthians 11:23-30).

2 The proper mode: For *baptism*, this is clearly a matter of immersion. The word itself is a transliteration of the Greek, *baptizo*, which means to immerse or plunge into. This is the manner in which Christ was baptized (Matthew 3:16). It was the manner of the disciples' baptisms (John 3:22-23). In fact, the picture of death, burial, and resurrection demands immersion (Romans 6:4). Additionally, the proper elements of the Lord's table are both the bread (unleavened, to represent the sinless body of Christ) and the juice of the vine (to represent Christ's sinless blood).

3 The proper understanding: Baptism is a picture of our total identification with Christ, His atoning work, and glorious resurrection. It is an expression of our belief that salvation is His work and, like His resurrected life, complete and eternal in nature. The Lord's table is a continuous reminder of Christ's death and His imminent return: "For as often as you eat this bread and drink the cup, you proclaim the Lord's death until He comes" (1 Corinthians 11:26). There is no specific instruction regarding the frequency that the Lord's table is to be observed. Most churches have generally chosen to observe it often enough that it remains a potent factor in church health and not so often that it becomes a mindless ritual for its participants.

4 The proper authority: The ordinances are public expressions; they preach a message. The message they preach is one consistent with the beliefs of the church authorizing baptism. Thus, in the understanding of church authority that unfolds for us in the New Testament, Peter asked the representatives of the Jerusalem church, who apparently accompanied him to the house of Cornelius, the centurion, "Surely no one can refuse the water for these to be baptized who have received the Holy Spirit just as we did, can he?" (Acts 10:47) If a local church does not feel that a candidate's beliefs are in concert with its own, it should resolve that issue before granting participation. It is obvious in Scripture that, in addition to the profession of the candidate, there is an obligation on the part of the church; otherwise Paul was overstepping his bounds in his instructions to the Corinthian church (See 1 Corinthians 11).

5 The proper life: Both baptism and the Lord's table are to be observed by individuals whose lives portray a consistent appreciation of grace and adherence to Scripture. When the eunuch asked Philip if he could be baptized, Philip responded by clarifying the eunuch's confession of faith (Acts 8:36-37). Likewise, in Paul's lengthy treatment of the issue of the Lord's table (1 Corinthians 11), he called for an intense, personal examination and cautioned that there could be severe consequences for the failure to do so.

Bill and his friend pored over the notes for almost an hour as Bill carefully answered each question by turning to the associated Scripture reference, reading, and explaining it. When Bill had completed his explanation of the fifth prerequisite for the proper observance of an ordinance, his friend sat back in his chair, deep in thought. Bill waited—and prayed.

"I want to be baptized," said his friend, almost startling Bill by his decisive tone of voice. "And then I want to participate in the Lord's Supper. Are you willing to help me do this?

"But what about the church?" Bill's friend continued. "Where is there a church in this city?"

"I haven't found one, as yet," Bill responded, "but I have some good news for you. Before I left my home country to come here, my church family met and prayed together that God would make my journey a success. The entire congregation also stood to say that if I should meet someone who would come to Christ, and should that person desire baptism, they would authorize me to do so. Further, they agreed to consider that new believer as part of their church family until a church was found or formed in his community.

"I can baptize you," said Bill, a smile breaking across his face, "and after that, the two of us can observe the Lord's Supper."

"Where can we do this," Bill's friend asked enthusiastically, "and when?"

"What about this Saturday evening?" asked Bill. "And we'll do it in my apartment. In fact, we might just consider that as our first worship service together."

Seated in his apartment later than evening, Bill decided to call Chris Foster with the good news regarding his friend.

"Do you realize how early it is?" asked Chris, obviously awakened by the call.

"Sorry," said Bill, "but I have a favor to ask."

"And the favor is?" Chris was fully awake now and eager to talk with Bill.

"Nothing much," said Bill, attempting to sound nonchalant. "It's just that when you get to church next Sunday morning, I'd like you to ask a few of my friends who are 'in the know' to pray for me and my friend. Your 'mission' over here will be having its first full worship service, complete with a baptism and the Lord's Supper.

Anyway, I just thought you'd like to know. I can tell you're still in bed, so we can talk later."

"Wait!" Chris almost shouted. "Don't you have time to tell me about it now?"

Bill thought for a moment, slid to the floor, and plugged in the battery charger before responding.

"All the time in the world for you, my friend."

Chapter Seven Review

And Jesus came up and spoke to them, saying, 'All authority has been given to Me in heaven and on earth. Go therefore and make disciples of all the nations, baptizing them in the name of the Father and the Son and the Holy Spirit, teaching them to observe all that I commanded you; and lo, I am with you always, even to the end of the age.' (MATTHEW 28:18-20)

Leading a friend to Christ is a privilege to be sought and treasured. It is *not* a responsibility to be hurried at the expense of doctrinal clarity or convictional certainty. A significant aspect of the Great Commission involves teaching followers of Christ to *observe*, or to *do*, all that Christ commanded those who followed Him during His lifetime. The New Testament pattern shows that the ordinance of baptism and the Lord's Supper are to follow one's conversion once a clear understanding is established.

The following outline will help in communicating doctrinal truth related to the ordinances:

What Should I Say to my Friend about Baptism and the Lord's Supper?

The meaning of ordinances

The establishment of ordinances

The proper observance of ordinances
Candidate
Mode
Understanding
Authority
Lifestyle

... *'Look! Water! What prevents me from being baptized?' And Philip said, 'If you believe with all your heart, you may.'* (Acts 8:36b-37a)

What Should I Say to my Friend When I am at a Loss for Words?

Chapter Eight

So I sent for you immediately, and you have been kind enough to come. Now then, we are all here present before God to hear all that you have been commanded by the Lord. (ACTS 10:33)

"I AM SORRY. IT WILL NOT WORK FOR ME TO COME to your apartment this evening." The voice of Bill's friend was matter-of-fact, so much so that, for a moment, he didn't recognize the caller.

"Excuse me?" Bill protested. "Who is this?"

"Bill, it is your friend. Can you not understand me?"

"Oh—well—what did you say? I'm not sure I heard what you said."

A gnawing sense of disillusionment and fear began to crawl into Bill's heart from somewhere deep within. He wondered again if he had heard his friend correctly. Everything had seemed so certain earlier in the week. Bill had been so excited that he'd scarcely studied for the exam, taking the fact that he'd passed it as the smile of God on his efforts. But the phone call changed everything.

"I do not think it would be best to come to your apartment for the baptism," his friend repeated. Bill attempted to gather his thoughts.

"Why?" Bill asked, "Has something happened? Are you all right? Is there a problem? Something I need to do?"

"No, my friend, no problem at all, except one."

"And what is that?" Bill's tone was urgent.

"I think we have a problem with room."

"The room? You mean my apartment?"

"No, we have a problem with room! You know—space."

"What are you talking about?" Bill was exasperated.

"Well, my friend, it seems you do not have enough room in your apartment. I have told my father and brothers about the baptism, and they are very interested. In fact, they have so many questions I cannot answer them. They are wondering if you would come to a dinner Sunday evening and tell them some of what you have told me—just a little. I know there is not so much time. But then we can have the baptism in my home. So, what do you think?

"Bill? Bill? My friend, are you there?"

Afterword

WOULDN'T IT BE GREAT IF EVERY WITNESSing experience were as simple, systematic, and straightforward as Bill's? That's rarely the case, of course, but some issues do remain constant. Bill's readiness to witness, even in the initial days of his overseas experience, is commendable, as was his genuine concern and diligent approach to the most vital and important message any of us have to share, the message of Christ.

Bill's determination to lead his friend along the path of genuine discipleship, rather than to simply evoke an outward decision, is also worth noting. The constraints of time and life often allow for only brief encounters, and we should be prepared to share the Gospel in such settings. As mentioned at the beginning of this book, there is a definite sense of urgency in our mission. With the New Testament's focus on both evangelism *and* church planting, it is always appropriate to prayerfully discern how best to encourage a decision of repentance and faith, asking God to give us wisdom as we look for clarity and conviction in the heart of the one with whom we are sharing the Gospel.

It is important to understand that the manner in which Bill dealt with his friend is not a call for delay in urging others toward repentance and faith. Instead, it was by the use of this approach that we were allowed to consider the various doctrinal questions that might surface in our conversations with others. Of course, men and women are not generally brought to faith by being on the losing side of a doctrinal argument. Rather, they must come face to face with God and be left with eternity in view. This is why the interchanges between Bill and his friend relied heavily on the use of questions, a method often employed by the Master Himself.

Peter encouraged us to be always "ready to make a defense to everyone who asks you to give an account for the hope that is in you" (1 Peter 3:15). Bill's own experience with God's saving grace, and the thorough manner by which his church family sought to disciple him, should stir each of us to a similar, passionate approach to the Christian life. Bill's own friend and his church back home partnered with him in his evangelistic adventure. Shouldn't we do the same with our believing friends and church family?

Bill knew that every believer is co-missioned by Christ (Matthew 28:18-20). That commission, the *Great Commission,* has little to do with geography and everything to do with our responsibility. As we are going, we are to fulfill the Lord's commission.

In the end, it is our loving obedience to the Lord who has saved us and our burden for the lost that compel us to share the Good News of Jesus. An honest atheist once asked the Christian community, "If you really believe what you say you believe, how much would you have to hate a person *not* to seek to make him a convert?"

Do you have a friend who has yet to repent and believe in Christ? Does your friend have questions about your faith? Isn't it time for you to ask …

What should I say to my friend?

Group Discussion Questions

Chapter One

1. What did you learn from this chapter that was particularly helpful?
2. How comfortable do you feel speaking with others about the nature of God?
3. Based on the discussion of Romans 11:36, what is your understanding of God?
4. What are evidences in your own culture that people have a non-biblical view of God?
5. Read Romans 1, then discuss the reasons why people have such twisted views of God.
6. Does God allow people to come to Him on their terms or only on His terms?
7. How accessible is God to you? What hinders your relationship with Him?
8. State the alliterative points to remember, which start with "R," from this chapter.
9. Memorize Romans 11:36.

Chapter Two

1. What is something new you learned from this chapter?
2. Who is the author of the Bible?
3. Is the Bible *the* Word of God, or does some of it simply *contain* the Word of God?
4. In its original manuscripts, were the words in the Bible inspired or just the thoughts?
5. How seriously should any Christian be about studying the Bible?
6. How is the Bible communicated to people who do not read?
7. Is there an advantage for an unbeliever to read the Bible?
8. State the alliterative points to remember, which start with "G," from this chapter.
9. Memorize 2 Timothy 3:16-17.

Chapter Three

1. Why was it important for Bill to explain about sin to his friend?
2. Do the sins we commit cause us to *be* sinners? Give evidence to the fact that we *are* sinners?
3. How is our sin nature somehow related to the sin of Adam in the Garden of Eden?
4. When the Bible speaks of the "wages of sin" as "death," what does that mean?
5. What separates us from God: the amount of our sin or the existence of sin in us?
6. Is there any way sinful mankind can earn good standing with God?
7. Do you recall the time in your life when you first became aware that you were a sinner?
8. State the alliterative points to remember, which start with "C," from this chapter.
9. Memorize 1 Corinthians 15:22.

Chapter Four

1. Did you learn something new about Jesus in Chapter Four or were you reminded of an important fact about Him?
2. Can you name several areas of the Christian life that depend on faith?
3. How is repentance linked to faith?
4. Is faith primarily a matter of thought? Emotion? Acting on the revealed will of God?
5. Where is the will of God most clearly revealed?
6. Is believing that Jesus exists the same as believing in Him?
7. When did you begin to follow Jesus as your personal Savior?
8. State the alliterative points to remember, which start with "P," from this chapter.
9. Memorize 1 Peter 3:18.

Chapter Five

1. After reading this chapter, why is it important to be able to explain "faith" to a nonbeliever?
2. Where did God first reveal that there was a Savior for mankind?

3. How did God prepare the heart of mankind through history to receive a Savior?
4. Why was it important that Jesus be born of a virgin? That He be sinless? That He die?
5. What did Jesus mean when He cried out "It is finished?"
6. Why is Jesus the only way to eternal life?
7. State the alliterative points to remember, which start with "N," from this chapter.
8. Memorize Hebrews 11:1-2.

Chapter Six

1. After reading this chapter, how would you define the church?
2. Why do you think the primary emphasis on the church in the New Testament is in its local sense?
3. Do you think it is important for every believer to be part of a local church? Why?
4. In what way(s) are you faithfully fulfilling your responsibility as a member of a local church?
5. On the mission field, what should we most emphasize? Evangelism? Church planting? Why?
6. What positive contribution does your church provide to your Christian life?
7. What are the alliterative points to remember, which start with "B," from this chapter.
8. Memorize Ephesians 1:22-23.

Chapter Seven

1. Did you learn something new in this chapter and if so, what?
2. What is an "ordinance," and what is its purpose?
3. What role does the church play in the proper observance of an ordinance?
4. Are ordinances necessary for salvation? If not, why do we observe them?
5. What were your thoughts and intentions when you were baptized? When you observe the Lord's Supper?
6. Can you name the five prerequisites for the proper observance of an ordinance?
7. Have you properly observed the ordinance of baptism? The Lord's Supper?
8. Memorize Matthew 28:18-20.

Chapter Eight

1. What has this story about Bill and his friend taught you about how to share your faith?
2. Share an example of a recent witnessing experience in which you applied the principles learned from this book.
3. Have you gained confidence in sharing your faith, whether in your normal environment or in a different culture, as a result of this study? How?
4. Review the alliterative points to remember from chapters one through six.
5. Review the five prerequisites for the proper observance of an ordinance.

Other books by Tom Elliff

Praying for Others

The Pathway to God's Presence

America on the Edge

A Passion for Prayer

In Their Own Words (with R.G. Witty)

*Unbreakable: The Seven Pillars
of a Kingdom Family*

Come Home to the Heart of God

Letters to Lovers

*Ten Questions Every Husband Should
Ask His Wife Every Year*

The Red Feather